Freudian Slips

Critical Perspectives on Women and Gender

Critical Perspectives on Women and Gender brings books on timely issues and controversies to an interdisciplinary audience. The series explores gender-related topics and illuminates the issues involved in current debates in feminist scholarship and across the disciplines.

Series Editorial Board

Ruth Behar
Müge Göçek
Carol Karlsen
Patricia Simons
Domna Stanton
Abigail Stewart
Christina Brooks Whitman

Titles in the series

Michelle Fine
Disruptive Voices: The Possibilities of Feminist Research

Susan D. Clayton and Faye J. Crosby
Justice, Gender, and Affirmative Action

Janice Doane and Devon Hodges
From Klein to Kristeva: Psychoanalytic Feminism and the Search for the "Good Enough" Mother

Jill Dolan
Presence and Desire: Essays on Gender, Sexuality, Performance

Judith Newton
Starting Over: Feminism and the Politics of Cultural Critique

Jill G. Morawski
Practicing Feminisms, Reconstructing Psychology: Notes on a Liminal Science

Mary S. Gossy
Freudian Slips: Woman, Writing, the Foreign Tongue

Freudian Slips

WOMAN, WRITING, THE FOREIGN TONGUE

Mary S. Gossy

Ann Arbor

THE UNIVERSITY OF MICHIGAN PRESS

Copyright © by the University of Michigan 1995
All rights reserved
Published in the United States of America by
The University of Michigan Press
Manufactured in the United States of America
⊗ Printed on acid-free paper

1998 1997 1996 1995   4 3 2 1

A CIP catalogue record for this book is available from the British Library.

Library of Congress Cataloging-in-Publication Data

Gossy, Mary S., 1959–
    Freudian slips : woman, writing, the foreign tongue / Mary S.
Gossy.
        p.   cm. — (Critical perspectives on women and gender)
    Includes bibliographical references.
    ISBN 0-472-09593-5 (alk. paper). — ISBN 0-472-06593-9 (pbk. :
alk. paper)
    1. Freud, Sigmund, 1856–1939. Zur Psychopathologie des
Alltagslebens. 2. Parapraxis. 3. Psychology, Pathological.
4. Psychoanalysis and feminism. I. Title. II. Series.
BF175.5.P35G67   1995
150.19'52—dc20   95-7758
                                                              CIP

For M. D. G. 1929–91

Freud was terrified of train travel, but my mother loved it. I commute in and out of New York from the wreck of what was a monumental Pennsylvania Station. There are remnants of the old building in the present broken subterranean shell—thick brass railings, dented but still shining; flying staircases that used to reach up under a glass canopy but now bump a warren of pipes and low ceilings. Before she died I asked my mother what it used to be like to leave Allentown and then arrive at the glamorous old Penn Station. I asked her this on a day when my father was driving us into New York and my mother was gazing in delight at a view she had somehow never seen before, from an approach she had never taken, lower Manhattan glimmering in the August heat like mother-of-pearl. She kept her eyes on the skyline on the other side of the water and only said, "You knew you were coming into a great city."

Acknowledgments

Lisa Dunn, Michael Berthold, and Myra Klein helped me sustain the effort of writing this book. All three gave generously of emotional, intellectual, and psychoanalytic support.

Jerry Aline Flieger encouraged me to turn a slip article into a slip book.

Thank you to my father and sister and Lisa and Michael for teaching me over and over again that home is a highway and as steady as a mountain.

Contents

Introduction

This book comes from error and anger. The error part is the easier of
the two to explain, so let me start there. In 1990 I was invited to
contribute an essay to a collection on the relationship of psychoanalytic theory to the works of Cervantes. One of the editors of the volume suggested that I pick up where I had left off in the last chapter
of a book I had published the year before. When I went back to look
over that old chapter for some new ideas, I was shocked to discover
that I had misread a very obvious meaning in the text at hand. Two
men had stolen a prostitute from police custody; the one man wanted
to rape her, since it had cost him so much trouble to get her, but the
second man would not let him. The first man said, "All right then, I'll
marry her, and then you won't be able to prevent me from doing
what I will with her."[1] He did marry her, we assume he got his way,
and that is the end of the story. It is all perfectly clear in the Spanish
text and in the translations. But I misread what happened. I thought
that the second man, the one who tried to prevent the rape, was the
one who married the girl. Despite my knowledge of feminist theory,
it was (at the time) impossible for me to read the obvious, which was
that in this case a young woman was forced to marry her would-be
rapist.

The essay that I wrote for the collection was an attempt to analyze
the psychological and political reasons for my misreading. In psychoanalytic terms this misreading qualifies as a Freudian slip, or a parapraxis, because its source is not ignorance but, rather, a repression.
For various reasons, despite the fact that the words were staring me
in the face, I could not accept their meaning.

From that essay I learned that, in political terms, the slip marks
the undertow of an opposing political current and the point at which
allegiance to opposing values has its strongest hold. For me the inabil-

ity to read *rapist* and *husband* together was tied to interpretations of the book that I had been taught in graduate school and marked my allegiance to an "old-boy" network from which I wanted to claim lineage—my identity as a radical feminist be damned. My slip showed me where orthodoxy was holding me back and interrupting my radical discourse.

A colleague at Rutgers, inquiring after my progress on the article, suggested that I take a look at the whole *Psychopathology of Everyday Life* by Sigmund Freud and write a book about it. At the time I was also considering doing a theoretical study of representations and responses to feminist pornography, but it was suggested to me by several people that such a book might not be the best project for a yet-to-be tenured assistant professor. So, I ended up writing this book on slips, which is, paradoxically, the more orthodox of the two projects.

Like the essay on misreading, *Freudian Slips: Woman, Writing, the Foreign Tongue* is an inquiry into the political implications of the slip, but it has a much broader context. It is an analysis of *The Psychopathology of Everyday Life* not only from a theoretical but also a textual perspective. It discusses how Freud writes about slips and what that writing can teach us about authority, teaching, theory, home, and what is foreign.

The Psychopathology of Everyday Life is a compendium of anecdotes that recount how slips happen. It is one of the most popular, in all senses of the word, of Freud's books. He stipulates that it is for the general reader and is not a theoretical text. Not by theorizing but by the endless hammering of its more than two hundred examples, in eleven editions and translations into at least twelve languages (in Freud's lifetime), it hopes to demonstrate the existence and mode of functioning of the unconscious in language. My first nightmarish task was to try to find a way to organize the study, given that it would be impossible (for me) to do a close reading of every example. What I discovered was that the majority of the anecdotes in the book are about slips that were committed in reference to a woman's body, some fixed written text, or the words of (what was to the person making the slip) a foreign language.

These female bodies, these texts, and these foreign tongues are, in *The Psychopathology of Everyday Life*, identified with a feminized unconscious that threatens authoritative discourse. *The Psychopathology of Everyday Life* was written to prove, authoritatively, that such an unconscious exists. But, as Freud points out, slips are contagious. The feminized slipperiness of woman, writing, and the foreign tongue constantly interrupts and upends the authoritative writing of *The Psychopathology of Everyday Life* and jostles the book's attempts to define and limit the slip. In anecdote after anecdote Freud, often in dialogue with a colleague "of academic background," attempts to analyze slips and to show how they work to reveal repressed content. But, in the act of writing about slips, the book shows how theory itself slips, and does so most graphically, when it insists upon the dominance of masculine over feminine and native over foreign. The more the text seeks to control or eradicate difference, the more its own internal difference becomes readable.

The operations of the slip are terrifying to and disruptive of univocal authority. I have had to face the fact that, by virtue of the slip's contagiousness, my own writing about it is bound to slip, too. But another point that this book tries to make is that, given that slips are unavoidable, there are ways that we can learn from them. The acceptance, rather than the denial of the slip, can create a new pedagogy, a way of learning in which authority is not seen as absolute and in which a slip is an occasion for a new dialogue, rather than a moment of shame to be forgotten as soon as possible. The slip insists on ways of meaning that exceed existing power structures and makes multiple meanings available.

I also argue that the categories of woman, writing, and the foreign tongue, the terms by which Freud theorizes the slip, are not arbitrary but, rather, clearly mark the terms of the slip's political possibilities. Because of the way that it undoes gender relations, the slip helps to show not only that the dominance of masculine over feminine is a fiction but, beyond that, that dominance is an invention that has an insistent tendency to undermine itself. The slip marks not only the undertow of orthodoxy in radical discourses but also the disruptive currents in discourses that seek the stability of dominance. This dominance, whether sexual, academic, or political, is undone in the moment of slipping. *Freudian Slips* discusses how the reference to women's bodies by scientists who seek to objectify those bodies results in the feminization of the scientists themselves. It shows how the desire to assimilate the power of a culture's master texts, by quotation of and association with their canonical authors, wreaks havoc with the political motivations of members of the intelligentsia or academy who are both within and without approved social definitions. Finally, my study analyzes the relationship between the native and the foreign and demonstrates how the use of the foreign—in travel narratives or foreign languages—can seem to be a method of getting away but inevitably leads back "home."

I believe that the metaphor that dominates *The Psychopathology of Everyday Life* is that of the female body as foreign text. This metaphor informs every chapter of Freud's book and slips in especially where it is least invited. Each chapter of my book analyzes the persistence of this metaphor from a different angle. The first chapter begins by pointing out that Freud *misquoted* Goethe's *Faust* the first time he wrote down the epigraph for *The Psychopathology of Everyday Life*. I show that this slip takes place because of the slip in gender that characterizes Freud's relationship with his friend Wilhelm Fliess; bisexuality, as theoretical problem and as personal relationship, makes it difficult to write canonically, and correctly. A strangely embodied femininity invades Freud and Fliess's masculine correspondence and disrupts it. But this element, called *Sorge*, or Worry in *Faust*, points to a way of knowing and learning that other writers who have invoked its name (Heidegger and Derrida, in addition to Freud) have avoided, because *Sorge*, like the slip, worries the Faustian mind.

In the second chapter a man's worries about a more concrete female body disrupt his intellectual and political rhetoric. An academic man who is Freud's traveling companion laments the anti-Semitism that is blocking his career. He misquotes a part of the *Aeneid* in which Dido wishes for descendants who might avenge her upon Aeneas, and his slip leads to the unwelcome possibility that a foreign woman whom he met while on holiday might soon be providing him with a descendant he does not really want. In this anecdote the foreign is directly linked with a female body and a classic text. But the slipper's inability to identify himself with the fate of that foreign, feminized body derails his own political project, which is to fight anti-Semitism. The slip marks a place where a new kind of political practice might be invented, but in this instance that possibility is set aside because of a need to adhere to structures of patriarchal legitimacy. The plight of Freud's companion is similar to that of other people, like certain academicians, for example, who are both within and without power and whose political urges toward change and survival are often co-opted by a yearning for respectability. But this slip, too, is a sign of the possibility of the return of a radical repressed. When the friend quotes Dido, he is casting himself in the role of a woman who was abandoned by a traveling man. On some level an identification with the other has been acknowledged, if not mobilized.

One reason that it is so hard to identify consciously with the oppressed other (that which is foreign and feminized) is that the existing symbolic system makes it seem dangerous to do so. A heterosexual man has been taught that he will lose that which is most precious to him if he does not follow the rules. The problem is that the slip proves that it is impossible always to stay within the approved grammar. The third chapter of my book picks up from the possibly pregnant girlfriend of the *Aeneid* quotation and follows a series of references in *The Psychopathology of Everyday Life* to pregnant women, especially mothers, and their relationship to the meaning of the slip. These mothers often appear in Freud's writings on screen memories, and I analyze a series of them in which a boy child remembers (or can't remember) his mother's body, pregnant with an unwelcome sibling. In these cases, which have to do both with fetishism and pregnancy, the female body is textualized as if it were a letter of the alphabet that initially, at least, spells out the priority of the male. But pregnancy upsets the order of the alphabet of castration and displaces the phallus from its position at the origin of language. On one level the boys' memories of their mothers' pregnancies turn the mother tongue into a foreign language. On another level, that of the slip, the same memories suggest a knowledge of a female body before castration, a knowledge that makes the construct of masculinity uncomfortably full of unplanned meanings and makes the man who remembers aware of new etymologies for his experience.

The scary thing about the fourth chapter is that it shows that slips can happen in one's native tongue as well as in foreign languages. Freud and a new friend both misquote another of Goethe's poems, this one "The Bride of Corinth." The (male) friend cannot decide whether he is in the position of a bride or of a groom. In this case he is quoting the words of another (poetic, and thus foreign, words) as a way of participating in Freud's authoritative discourse—but what happens is that, in trying to accede to authority, he has slipped into a submissive position. Here and elsewhere in *The Psychopathology of Everyday Life* theory is a homoerotic dialogue among men that works very hard to exclude women. Yet that theory is built on constant reference to femininity, and the concrete reality of the female bodies that it represses insistently returns to undermine it. The slips that are narrated in *The Psychopathology of Everyday Life* show again and again that there is a female body that makes sense and whose insistent meanings exceed the definitions of a theoretical femininity.

The collision between a theoretical fantasy of femininity and the concrete experiences of female bodies inevitably brings us, in the fifth chapter, to the case of Dora, which Freud was writing at the same time as *The Psychopathology of Everyday Life.* Many people who have written on Dora have mentioned this fact, but no one has discussed what it might mean to the theory of the unconscious expounded in Freud's book on slips. *The Psychopathology of Everyday Life* was published immediately after Freud wrote it and went into eleven editions, ten of them "enlarged." The Dora case, on the other hand, was kept from publication for four years before it finally came out. Now, the anecdote is the fundamental structure of *The Psychopathology of Everyday Life,* and it is no coincidence that the etymology of the word *anecdote* is "that which is not published or given out." The overpublished, excessive book on slips, so full of anecdotes that it becomes fragmented, is a compensatory publication of the unpublished Dora case; *The Psychopathology of Everyday Life* is a hysterical embodiment of the repressed "Fragment of an Analysis of a Case of Hysteria."

According to his letters to Fliess, Freud was writing *The Psychopathology of Everyday Life* before, during, and after he was writing Dora. The "Fragment" might thus be read as a part of the book on slips. In fact, there is some direct intertextuality. In *The Psychopathology of Everyday Life* Freud tells a story about how he came to choose the name Dora for a patient whose case history he was writing. But, because of their relation to a slip that Freud's pupil Sandor Ferenczi reports, other anecdotes about hysterical girls make ever stronger connections between the two works. One day Ferenczi wrote *anektode,* instead of *anekdote,* in his journal. *Tode* is the German word for death, and Ferenczi's slip led me to an examination of the ways in which a living female body that exceeds the definitions of theory can be threatened with death by a theoretical discourse, the *anektode,* that will not learn its language.

Despite the real terrors that *anectodal* theorizing evokes, it is worth remembering the context of Ferenczi's slip. A Gypsy had been sentenced to death by hanging and asked as a last request to be able to choose the tree from which he would hang. Despite much searching, he never found an appropriate tree. The moral is that the Gypsy, as archetypal foreign other, offers a model of a rhetoric that is not silenced or murdered by existing laws. Part of my work at the end of chapter 5, and throughout *Freudian Slips*, is to suggest ways of writing theory that free, rather than sacrifice, the bodies of women.

The last part of the book, which is not a chapter but more of a conclusion and epilogue, is concerned with the writing hand of a woman and to what degree the pen in that hand is as murderous as any other. It is based on a dream in which I, a non–native Spanish speaker and professor of Spanish literature, tried to write that "all narrative has blood on its hands" in Spanish, on a blackboard. It tells the story of how living, writing, and reading through error, in contact with the blood of a female body that is not dying, can indicate a way to make sense beyond co-optation or silence. I try to suggest some positive ways that slips can be used to promote discourses that value difference (of all kinds, but especially sexual difference) instead of repressing or colonizing them.

Throughout this work I have been conscious not only of my slips and errors but also of an anger that is related to them. Not all errors are slips; slips are errors that you make when you know better, and for that reason they contain a hint of perversity, of willful deviation, of going where you want to go, instead of where the rules tell you to go. The whole of *The Psychopathology of Everyday Life* is full of travel stories and of slips that happen in or because of them—of people straying, erring, wandering, from their accustomed paths and then finding out things that they needed, but didn't want, to know. To err, to wander freely, is essential to knowledge. While I was writing this book, I often felt the need to wander, to get up out of my chair and walk the fifteen blocks to the bank or just around the park. I went out on the streets of the East Village in New York City the same literature professor and feminist theorist that I was when I was inside my apartment sitting at my desk. But theory did not matter to the violent discourses I encountered on my walks. In the thirty or so minutes that my identifiably female body moved autonomously through neighborhoods, good and bad, on the way to Union Square, every time, and more than once, men, visibly of all classes and races, subjected me to verbal assault. It was wintertime, and I was wearing heavy clothing and my habitual boots and jacket. I am six feet tall but otherwise not particularly noticeable. Nevertheless, at least two or three times on each walk, in each direction, men directed sexual comments at me. These locutions are familiar to women who do not spend most of their public time in automobiles or accompanied by a protective male; comments range from the disturbingly violent and obscene to the ridiculous. What made me angry about them was that they hemmed in my wandering. In response to them, I constantly found myself changing course, trying to figure out a way to move through the city without being bordered or defined by these words, which were impossible to ignore. It is possible not to respond and to pretend you don't hear what the man is saying, but it doesn't stop the words from reaching you. Similarly, it is possible to engage the man with some kind of comeback, but these usually backfire. It struck me that my position as a woman walking on the street and being harassed by this male discourse was analogous to the position of the feminist theoretician. How is it possible to make my own discourse in an environment that is overdetermined and controlled by another discourse that seeks to silence and override it?

I wanted a feminist theory that would change my experience on the streets of New York. Most academic feminist theory is singularly ineffective in this regard. The possibilities, from essentialism to the performance of gender, all require a large investment of energy *in response to* the dominant discourse. I, on the other hand, wanted that time and energy for myself and the people to whom I *choose* to respond. The men on the street do not care where I stand in reference to questions about the construction of gender. They simply see an identifiably female body on the move, and they want to detain it in its movement. They want to control the slippery female, too, and it makes me mad.

So, my question is, what kind of *practice* of difference can help me survive in my (culturally encoded) difference? My female body is the ground of my experiences in the civilized discourses of gender. It is a form of intelligible difference that has made me and is part of what I am now. Whether I identify with it or not, it determines the way that power acts out on me. I would like to continue to err in it, as it is. And at this point that is the only practice I can suggest: to keep on slipping. In this book I say that to slip, and to acknowledge the slip, will redirect the conscious discourse in which the slip occurs. Similarly, exposure to a foreign language will eventually make changes in a native tongue. A foreign word that many theoreticians use for political practice is *praxis;* this commonly known fact is of no special note, except that the word echoes in the technical English term for Freudian slip, which is *parapraxis.* Freud's word, *Fehlleistung,* has no equivalent in English, so his translator had to coin one. *Fehlleistung* means "faulty function"; *parapraxis* means, in this context, "doing incorrectly," but in terms of a political practice *parapraxis* has additional possibilities. *Para-* can mean "beside" and "beyond," as well as "incorrectly" and "similar to." A feminist parapraxis could be a way of continuing one's errant movement along the streets, of either the urban or the academic marketplace, not responding to and thus not detained by that which seeks to halt whatever self-determination is possible to a female body. In such a parapractic, or slippery, juxtaposition of two discourses, the dominant one cannot retain the same position it had before its contact with the slip. The insistent autonomous error that a visible, mobile, public female body represents should, theoretically, alter the language of domination. In *The Psychopathology of Everyday Life* it is possible to see, at any rate, how the bodies of women, as opposed to abstractions of femininity, slip through theoretical discourse and make their own impractical, parapractic kind of sense.

1

Borrowing Another's Words

FAUST: Is someone there?
WORRY: The question calls for Yes.
FAUST: Ist jemand hier?
SORGE: Die Frage fordert Ja!

—*Faust*, part 2, act 5, scene 5

Freud got the motto for *The Psychopathology of Everyday Life* from his friend Wilhelm Fliess. In his letter of 14 October 1900 he told Fliess:

> For the "Psychology of Everyday Life" I would like to borrow from you the nice motto, *Nun ist die Welt von diesem Spuk so voll.* . . . Otherwise I am reading Greek archaeology and reveling in journeys I shall never make and treasures I shall never possess.[1]

In light of what will become *The Psychopathology of Everyday Life,* two things about this citation are significant. First is the evolution of *Psychology* to *Psychopathology,* a change that occurs by 1 January 1901.[2] The new name is more congruent with Freud's belief that the difference between normal and neurotic mental life is a matter of degree, and not of kind; that the investigation of parapraxes—which are known now, in everyday parlance, as Freudian slips—shows "that the borderline between the normal and the abnormal in nervous matters is a fluid one, and that we are all a little neurotic."[3] The slip, for Freud, is relentless proof of the existence of the unconscious and of its operations everyday, in everyone. It is a way of legitimizing his claims for the unconscious on a universal level.

Freud, in 1900, was still very much in need of such legitimization. His work was often under attack or wholly misunderstood. He was conscious of and sensitive to the critical climate in general and in particular when he was contemplating the appearance of the first version of the book on parapraxes. His 9 June 1901 letter to Fliess says that

11

"Everyday Life" will appear in the July issue of the *Monatsschrift*. If I were to abstain from forming an opinion of my works, only your favorable opinion would be left.[4]

Insisting upon the neuroses of the general populace won Freud few allies, at least at the beginning of his career, and he needed to know that there was a friendly reader for his work. Unfortunately, Fliess was not entirely reliable in this respect. His marital problems in the summer of 1901 led him to implicate Freud in the difficulties he was having with his wife and to impugn Freud's analytic method with the bruising accusation that "the reader of thoughts merely reads his own thoughts into other people," a statement that Freud said "renders all my efforts valueless." "If that is what you think of me," he continued,

just throw my "Everyday Life" unread into the wastepaper basket. It is full of references to you—manifest ones, for which you supplied the material, and concealed ones, for which the motivation goes back to you. The motto, too, was a gift from you. Apart from anything that might remain of the content, you can take it as a testimonial to the role you have played for me up to now. Having announced it in this way, I feel I can send you the essay when it comes into my hands without further words.[5]

Personal and professional jealousy and intellectual disagreements undid the friendship between Freud and Fliess.[6] First, Ernst Kris, in his introduction to *The Origins of Psycho-Analysis*,[7] and, more recently, Jeffrey Masson, in his notes to the Freud-Fliess correspondence, have theorized about the causes and effects of the disintegration of the relationship on Freud personally and on psychoanalysis. But in terms of the function of the slip itself in writing, and its consequences for reading and writing, the utility of this biographical information is to highlight the notion of borrowing, the making the words of the other one's own.

In order to explain, I would like to return to the question of the motto "borrowed" from Fliess. The second significant point in the letter of 14 October 1900 is not that Freud got the quotation from Fliess, but that he got it wrong. The actual quotation from *Faust* runs,

Nun ist die Luft von solchem Spuk so voll,

[Now is the air so full of such haunting,]

not "Nun ist die Welt von diesem Spuk so voll... [Now is the world so full of this haunting...]."[8] Freud's letter, when it combines the slip with the use of ellipsis, creates a fragmented misquotation from *Faust*, which it proposes to use as the first words of the text of what will become *The Psychopathology of Everyday Life*. In that book two full chapters and numerous other examples are devoted to the examination of a specific form of parapraxis, that of the misquotation of famous pieces of literature by people who should know better, so it is striking that the motto—that is, the concentrated rhetorical essence of the book, its nuclear summary—should itself appear, however surreptitiously, by way of a slip. On one level the misquotation shows a variation on Harold Bloom's idea of the "anxiety of influence," since it indicates a need for legitimization based on conflicting desires to derive intellectual lineage from a great man and to claim absolute originality. Or the slip could be seen to make manifest a desire to be in Goethe's company, to speak not with the voice and paradoxical authority of Faust but, rather, with that of Faust's creator (a fantasy that may have been realized when Freud was awarded the Goethe Prize in 1930). Also, the error itself avoids or displaces the debt to the father who went before. The displaced authority, in this case, is not only Goethe but also Fliess. The slip in the Goethe quotation thus marks a failure to stay loyal to the structures of academic paternity and legitimacy.

On the textual, rather than the biographical, level the analysis of the slip has other related implications. The letter asks to "borrow" a quotation that, first of all, does not belong to Fliess, since it supposedly comes from a drama by Goethe, and, second, because of its inaccuracy, cannot even be said to belong to Goethe. The slip undoes the notion of authorship; it compromises the integrity of a classic text by disrupting its paternity. The author of the slip both participates in and disrupts the authoritative text and, in this case, does so as a consequence of the creation of a new book. The slip disturbs the authoritative text at its most elemental levels, those of the word and the letter. When quotations are mixed up, so are authority and attribution. The slip can show

how one text slides into, away from, around, and through others. It can illuminate the structures of writing that explicitly constitutes itself as analytical and critical—of the writing of others, of borrowed words.

Borrowed words are words that belong to someone else. In the example that I am discussing, the words that Freud seeks to borrow come from Goethe by way of Fliess. They are the words of an other, a text, through whom the borrower seeks to establish a relationship with a third person, who is somehow perceived to have a right to that authoritative text. They are words that need to pass through a form of translation—from Goethe to Fliess to Freud—before they can become Freud's own. As such, they are a kind of foreign language. One is more susceptible, as Freud says, to committing slips when using a foreign language than when employing one's native tongue. But sometimes miscommunication in a foreign tongue is preferable to any form of communication in one's original language. Sometimes a foreign tongue is the only one that will do. This is particularly true in questions of desire: the foreign tongue is someone else's tongue in my mouth.

To borrow words is both to assume the authority of the other and to avoid, to a certain extent, responsibility for what one is saying: I may have said it, but I said it in someone else's words. Because of the possibilities for displacement that are involved in the use of foreign words, they are ideal for discussing or referring to sexual desires that, however strongly they may be felt, may not be entirely acceptable to the party or parties they concern. As examples of this displacement of problematic sexual feelings into foreign languages, I would like to cite the frequent use, by sensitively tempered speakers of English, of French and Latin words and phrases to describe particular events and situations and even the general acceptance of the anglicized term *double entendre* as a way of flagging sexually inflected puns so that they may be obliquely referred to but certainly not ignored. By using the words of an other, a writer may project his or her unacceptable desires onto and through another body of discourse. This other discourse, embodied in a foreign tongue, can itself become a repository for the unwelcome desire operating between two or more people.

The quotation from Faust is such a repository. Freud did not need to ask Fliess for permission to quote Goethe. His work was and is part of a cultural patrimony that stretches from the lowest to the highest levels of German-speaking society. (I remember my paternal grandmother, a countrywoman who left a small village in Burgenland to become a seamstress in Budapest, where she sneaked into lectures at the university, reciting Goethe's poems from memory with a look of transport on her face.) When Freud asks Fliess to borrow Goethe's words, he must be asking for something other than those words, which are no more Fliess's than they are anybody's. The words of a canonical text become, here, an object of exchange between two men, an authoritative text that they can share and over which their relationship may take place. The quotation becomes a locus of men's (*homme*, in French) homosocial desire, or, in Luce Irigaray's term (in French a double entendre, of course), *hom(m)osexuality*, in which a woman (or a text or a territory or a car or some other feminized object) is used as a conduit for the prohibited homosexuality, or male-centered desire, between men.[9] In the case of Freud's relationship with Fliess this male homosocial desire is made explicit in the letter of 7 August 1901. The paragraph that follows the one I quoted earlier runs:

> As to Breuer, you are certainly quite right about *the* brother, but I do not share your contempt for friendship between men, probably because I am to a high degree party to it. In my life, as you know, woman has never replaced the comrade, the friend.[10]

Some years later Freud would confide to his biographer Ernest Jones that, regarding his feelings in reference to Fliess, "There is some piece of unruly homosexual feeling at the root of the matter."[11]

It is interesting in this regard to note that the specific problem of professional jealousy that disrupted Freud's and Fliess's relationship was connected to the question of bisexuality. Fliess had first told Freud that he believed that all human beings were bisexual in 1897, but by the summer of 1900 Freud had forgotten about Fliess's assertion, which he had originally disputed, and Freud was expressing the idea to Fliess as if it were Freud's invention. The incident appears in *The Psychopathology of Everyday Life* in chapter 7, "The Forgetting of Intentions and Impressions," in which Freud admits his mistake and also that "it is painful to be requested in this way to surrender one's originality" (144). The question of who came up with the idea first, and the fact that the submissive man (Freud) seeks to usurp the priority of the authoritative man (Fliess) by forgetting the facts, is certainly an oedipal one. Yet it is conceivable that the same difficulty might have arisen over any number of issues and questions that the two men had discussed over the years. But it is specifically the idea of bisexuality that generates first an unpleasantness and then, finally, a rift between the two men.

When he discusses the bisexuality slip in the public forum that is *The Psychopathology of Everyday Life* and also in the private correspondence with Fliess, Freud's manner is characteristically honest and clinical. But his rigorous self-analysis and openness are not enough to defuse the explosive potential that the notion of bisexuality, as a sexual constitution that by definition cannot always live up to the idealized constructs of a compulsory heterosexuality, can exercise over language. The awareness of an "unruly homosexual feeling" does not necessarily neutralize it, and the mere discussion of it, no matter how clinical, in a discourse organized by heterosexuality, will tend to disrupt that discourse. James Strachey and Ernest Jones both note that Freud got the date of his walk with Fliess wrong: it did not occur in the year that Freud puts it, 1901, but, rather, in 1900. Jones says that this is because 1901 was "a time when he [Freud] no longer met Fliess, but still wanted to."[12] After the misdated explanation of the bisexuality slip, Freud continues:

> Finding fault with one's wife, a friendship which has turned into its opposite, a doctor's error in diagnosis, a rebuff by someone with similar interests, *borrowing someone else's ideas*—it can hardly be accidental that a collection of instances of forgetting, gathered at random, should require me to enter into such distressing subjects in explaining them. (144; italics mine)

The idea of borrowing is connected to "distressing subjects." While the desire to borrow or the act of borrowing may not in themselves be symptomatic, an error in articulating that which is to be borrowed is. In this example a slip in the "correct" organization of relationships between men—that is, a slip-up in the heterosexual rules that determine what men are permitted to desire from one another—produces a slip in writing. The bisexuality parapraxis, carefully recounted but still erring inside the book, is announced outside the book, in the letter that asks for a literally unauthorized gift.

Here, as elsewhere in *The Psychopathology of Everyday Life*, it is evident that a parapraxis marks a slip of gender. Not only do parapraxes occur when gender slips, but, as I will show in the course of this study, both the theory and the text of *The Psychopathology of Everyday Life* depend upon, and are possible because of, slippages in orthodox gender structures. Not surprisingly, the strategy of canonical analysis of the slip itself, as a manifestation of unconscious content, is to feminize it in its relationship to the orderly, rational discourse in which it occurs. Slippage in a text is then materially constituted as difference.

This difference is evident in the two versions of the *Faust* quotation that Freud supplies:

Nun ist die Welt von diesem Spuk so voll

[Now is the world so full of this haunting]

and

Nun ist die Luft von solchem Spuk so voll

[Now is the air so full of such haunting][13]

The slip marks the space between the world and the air, and between *this* and *such*. In both cases the boundaries are unclear; for example, it is difficult to tell where the world ends and the air begins—where does earth slip into ether? The first version highlights a concreteness and a specificity that are absent from the second: that the world is full of this particular menace is a slightly more immediate expression than that the air is full of such and such a kind of threat. The indistinctness of Goethe's version is spookier though, because his haunting inhabits the air, which we inhale—the indefinite *Spuk* can enter us with our life's breath or is already part of it. The effect of this slip is to undo the binary opposition between *world* and *air*, to distress the distinction between material and spirit. The space between the terms is inhabited by the slip.

Perhaps *die Welt* crept into Freud's version from the line that precedes the quotation, in which Faust laments his quest for knowledge, and says that he was a man once, before he learned what he now knows:

Das war ich sonst, eh ich's im Dürsten suchte,
Mit Frevelwort mich und die Welt verfluchte.

[Once I was that, before I searched the gloom,
cursing myself and the world with iniquitous words.]

Analysis of a psyche or of writing in this context—that is, a context in which one seeks not self-knowledge but, rather, mastery over that which is perceived as other—has ended up feeling like a descent into the gloom, like a gradual process of self-damnation, or at least of convicting oneself with one's own words.

At this point in the drama Faust is near his end. Four sisters—Want, Guilt, Need, and Worry—have come to prepare the way for their brother, Death. Because Faust is a rich man, only one of the sisters, Worry, can enter his house. She is the haunting shape who blinds him just before he dies: Worry survives the omniscient investigator.

Similarly, *Spuk* is a word that survives the slippage between the two quotations. It is a noun that has no plural form, and it means "haunting, ghostly apparition, nightmare, ghastly business"—something amorphous and scary, that comes in uninvited. When combined with the identity specified in *Faust*, that of Worry, *Spuk* becomes analogous to the ever-unwelcome manifestations of the repressed. The errors in the first quotation, as well as its preservation of *Spuk*'s integrity, only serve to emphasize the continuity of the presence of the anxiety-bearing, haunting shape.

It is not inconsequential that this shape should embody a feminine being. *Spuk* is a masculine noun in German, but such materiality as there is of *Spuk* in *Faust* is feminine: it refers to a community of four sisters whose job it is to undo Faust, the mastermind. When the quotation becomes an epigraph to *The Psychopathology of Everyday Life*, which is a study of the unwelcome eruptions of the repressed into language, of the haunting of discourse by the repressed, *Spuk* may be understood as *slip*, as a feminine interloper in the purportedly masculine realms of grammar, meaning, and the conscious. After listening to the four sisters talk among themselves, Faust says,

Den Sinn der Rede konnt ich nicht verstehn.

[The sense of their speaking I cannot understand.]

but then he goes on to paraphrase, quite accurately, what he has just heard. Like anyone else caught in a slip, he understands its meaning all too well but displaces the responsibility for this understanding onto someone or something else, the discourse of a feminized other.

The feminization of the slip in *The Psychopathology of Everyday Life* is the result of a slip in gender. *Spuk*, the amorphous haunting thing, may be a masculine noun, but it is concretely engendered in the text as feminine. The female becomes a context through which the slip is told and analyzed. *The Psychopathology of Everyday Life* is thus written under the rubric of slipped gender. It is told literally under the authority of a quotation from *Faust* that started out as a misquotation: *The Psychopathology of Everyday Life* is a book about slips written by way of a book that slipped. Finally, it is a book profoundly influenced by and produced by means of the borrowing of the words of an other (and of the many others who contributed examples of their own slips to the book's eleven editions). It is constituted by means of a foreign language—that is, by words that are not one's own. The story of slips in *The Psychopathology of Everyday Life* is told by means of more than two hundred anecdotes, the majority of them narrated over the bodies of women or texts and foreign words that have been subjected to a process of connotative feminization. This study explores the relationship of woman, writing, and the foreign tongue and why it is that they are seemingly indispensable to the elaboration of a theory of the existence of the unconscious and its emergence into language.

Near the end of the essay "Freud and the Scene of Writing," Jacques Derrida suggests the question of

a *psychopathology of everyday life* in which the study of writing would not be limited to the interpretation of the *lapsus calami,* and, moreover, would be more attentive to this latter and to its originality than Freud himself ever was. "*Slips of the pen,* to which I now pass, are so closely akin to slips of the tongue that we have nothing new to expect from them" (XV, 69). This did prevent Freud from raising the fundamental juridical problem of responsibility, before the tribunal of psychoanalysis, as concerns, for example, the murderous *lapsus calami* (ibid.).[14]

A *lapsus calami* is a slip of the pen. In *The Psychopathology of Everyday Life* the slipping pen is murderous only in regard to women; Derrida is referring in this quotation to a series of anecdotes that recount how a doctor repeatedly wrote orders for overdoses of drugs for elderly women (122–25). Only chance prevented the deadly prescriptions from being administered. In another anecdote Freud mixes up two bottles of medications that he is applying to an old woman's eyes and is horrified by his mistake (177–78). I discuss these examples in detail later.[15] For the moment I want to take Derrida's suggestion further and to use an analysis of the book on slips to raise the problem of responsibility in reference not only to psychoanalysis but also to the practice and practitioners of critical theory in general. Theory and analysis carried out over the body of woman have effects beyond the boundaries of the text, on real women's bodies. We can be sure that no anecdotes about prescriptions for *fatal* overdoses that *were* administered to women appear in *The Psychopathology of Everyday Life*. But the written slip, as record, provides a means of tracing the structures of theory and their effects on feminized others.

The anecdotes that appear in *The Psychopathology of Everyday Life*—whether they are about slips of the tongue, bungled actions, forgetting, or the other kinds of parapraxes—have in common with the ones about slips of the pen the fact that they are, in the book, codified as writing. Regardless of the circumstances of its occurence, the *Freudian* slip is a written one. Parapraxis as theory and as event is textualized. This idea has at least two implications for "*a psychopathology of everyday life* in which the study of writing would not be limited to the interpretation of the *lapsus calami*." First, it breaks down the apparent distinctions between slips of the pen and slips of the tongue: both of these, as well as the other kinds of slips, are translated into writing in Freud's book. The written narration of the slip thus becomes the ground of its analysis. Second, the definition of slip as *written* entity suggests, like Derrida, a much broader symptomatology of writing than what *The Psychopathology of Everyday Life* has to say about slips of the pen. This study concerns itself with Freud's writing on and of all kinds of parapraxes.

"Freud and the Scene of Writing" first appeared in English in 1978. Aside from Derrida's suggestion at the end of that essay, remarkably little attention has been paid to either the idea of the slip or to *The Psychopathology of Everyday Life*, despite the fact (or perhaps because of it) that, of all of Freud's works, it is the one that most explicitly discusses the ways that language, and written language in particular, is traduced by the repressed. The critical approaches to the text that have appeared have either used it to attack Freudian analytic methodology or to inform studies of other works. The Italian Marxist critic Sebastiano Timpanaro, in 1976, and James Guetti, in 1988, have similar responses to the text, with Guetti's article echoing Timpanaro's book in many respects, except for that of class analysis. Both men call Freud's methodology into question and state that his formulation of a relationship between the slip and the unconscious is an example of circular logic or of illogic.[16] Timpanaro does so on the basis of comparisons with textual criticism (the branch of philology that deals with errors of transcription and quotation in manuscripts) and seeks to prove that slips do not manifest the existence of an unconscious but are, rather, mechanical abberations that do not necessarily have any psychic significance for the person who produces them. Guetti sees a tautology in Freud's understanding of the slip-unconscious relationship:

> The significance one might assign to a slip of the tongue cannot logically be justified until the unconscious is established as its source. And the existence of the unconscious as a separate mental faculty cannot be proved unless faulty acts of speaking or other behavior already have a sense yet to be derived from it. (40)

What strikes me as interesting about both writers is the vehemence of their insistence upon the idea that slips do not mean anything. Anyone who has had the misfortune of uttering a slip during an argument, and thus losing a position of rhetorical superiority, or of writing a slip that somehow compromised one's authority or credibility knows that a theory of the unconscious is not necessary to appreciate the eruption of meaning that a slip represents: all that is necessary is a reader or listener who takes the slip at its literal value. *Unconscious* is the word that psychoanalysis uses to define one of the currents contributing to the slip's meaning. Nevertheless, the slip has meaning for people who have never heard of the unconscious or who do not accept the theory of its existence. An awareness of the meaningfulness of slips antedates any Freudian theory of them by several centuries.[17]

Both Timpanaro and Guetti see Freud's way of interpreting slips as inventing or inserting meaning where there was none or supplanting a preexistent meaning. The former says that Freud's "is an effort to penetrate *at all times* to an underlying, unpleasant reality arrived at only by dint of a victory over the subject's resistances" (179); Guetti thinks that Freud's version of slips wants to "reveal... and provide access to a state of mind or a sequence of meanings truer than the one they interrupt" (37). Neither critic mentions that the slip does not need anyone to call attention to it: it is usually glaring and if invisible, is so only to the person who produced it. On 23 October 1992, at a rally in New Jersey, then President George Bush began a sentence by saying "I hate to ruin a lovely recession—I mean reception. . . ." The slip was reported on the local television news and appeared the next evening in the "Weekend Update" news parody on "Saturday Night Live."[18] Its meaning, as I have mentioned, is not the result of elaborate interpretive processes but, rather, of its literalness, and, it is important to note, it has political implications, which Bush tried to ignore but which "Saturday Night Live" emphasized.

In somewhat different circumstances I gave a paper before a very large audience at the university where I earned my doctorate. I was doing a psychoanalytic reading of some lesbian pornographic images and wanted to show how lesbian desire differs from heterosexual desire, particularly in relationship to castration. But I was anxious about the presentation and found that the question I most wanted to avoid (because it challenged my academic mastery of the situation) inserted itself most inopportunely: I loudly proclaimed the word *phallus* in the middle of a sentence in which it did not comfortably fit. But, of course, the word was crucial, if until that point unavailable, to the public discussion, and, because the slip was acknowledged rather than ignored, it changed the rest of the session's discourse. My point here is that the meaning of the intrusion of the word need not be painfully extracted: it is evident on the literal level. Acknowledging the political importance of a slip produces a different succeeding discourse than does pretending it never happened.

Similarly, contrary to what Timpanaro and Guetti say, the interpretation of the slip does not have to be seen as "truer" than or competitive with the discourse that it interrupts. A slip does not only mean something else; instead, it means *with* the discourse it appears in. My *phallus* slip is relevant here, because it shows, paradoxically, how slips displace what some theorists have called the phallocentric way of reading and writing—a way that seeks single meanings and erases the participation of an unconscious in the making of discourses. It is interesting to note that neither Timpanaro nor Guetti tests Freud's method on themselves. Both authors can only see analysis, and psychoanalysis in particular, as a method for the domination of others. I am aware that psychoanalytic theory has been used to excuse or enfranchise the domination of subordinate groups, such as women and gay people of both sexes. But that does not mean that it cannot be a powerful tool for liberation as well. Its particular utility is in terms of self-criticism. Those who take exception to Freud's interpretive methods might start with "Constructions in Analysis," a late essay that suggests that the analysand's emotional affect in response to a construction offered by an analyst may be the best gauge of the construction's accuracy.[19] The vehemence of the texts that I have been discussing here, and their investment in showing Freud to be "absurd," "obviously illogical," "amusing," "extreme," "ludicrous," "embarrassing" (these adjectives are from Guetti's article, but similar ones appear in Timpanaro's book as well), seems, at the least, misplaced. But, if Freud's theory of the meaning of slips is conceived of as an unwelcome challenge to notions of linguistic, psychic, or political mastery, then the emotional response is more understandable. At any rate, it is interesting to note how criticisms of Freud's method echo Fliess's comment (cited on page 12) that "the reader of thoughts merely reads his own thoughts into other people's." Such critical reactions seem based in a need to determine which man will own mastery over interpretation.

In readings that are more open to psychoanalysis Anthony Wilden and Jane Gallop look at the slip in terms of the question "Who is speaking?" in it and do so precisely to raise the issue of mastery.[20] But for these two authors Freud's work on slips—specifically, the "Signorelli" example from the first chapter of *The Psychopathology of Everyday Life*—is used as way of beginning to discuss Lacan. Freud's text is set aside in favor of Lacan's. Also, the problematics of using the phrase "Who is speaking?" in reference to *written* language about the slip are not addressed in either text, and neither is Freud's writing about slips—that is, there is no inquiry into the rhetoric and representation of slips in Freud's textual discourse. Lacan's reading of Freud is analyzed, but the Freudian text is not approached directly. Additionally, when *The Psychopathology of Everyday Life* is mentioned it is not considered on its own but, rather, as part of a trio of books, with *The Interpretation of Dreams* and *Jokes and Their Relation to the Unconscious.* Thus, when Shoshona Felman writes about the slippery, and slipping, in *The Literary Speech Act,*[21] she does so in relation to *Jokes.* In that book, according to Felman, humor and slipping go together, making of the discursive moment in question a pratfall. This kind of slipping (as on a banana peel) is intentional, or appropriated as intentional. The distinction between a joke and a parapraxis is that the joke is produced intentionally and intends an effect upon its hearer or reader. A joke, like a dream interpretation, is a form of conscious rhetorical mastery of problematic wishes or feelings. Jokes and dreams highlight the originality and cleverness of their authors. A successful joke teller gains mastery over others, by producing laughter in them. The joke as text is a tool of rhetorical domination.

In analytical terms the dream as text plays a passive role analogous to the joke's active one. It may function as a text from which previously unconscious meanings may be extracted, but that meaning awaits the dreamer's willing attention. Dreams rarely force their meaning upon the dreamer. While dreaming itself cannot be called intentional, the psychoanalytic accession to the unconscious meaning of dreams is. Thus, in both the case of jokes and of dreams the joke teller or dreamer becomes a willing participant in the production of meaning and, in both cases, does so in order to gain mastery—over an audience or (by way of interpretation) over a dream text.

A Freudian slip's power to disrupt language and social relations comes from the fact that it is more than a thought; it is always the result of an embodied *action.* Unlike a dream, which can be kept to oneself, a slip insists on itself, inevitably in the presence, actual or impending, of another person. It cannot be hidden. At the moment of slipping one's fluency in the manipulation of signs and language is called into question. Either there is too much or not enough meaning— the only thing that is certain is that one is not producing the effects that one had consciously intended to produce. Perhaps this is one reason for the lack of attention paid to *The Psychopathology of Everyday Life* by literary critics and theorists. It makes too obvious the fragility of authorship, authority, and intentionality and does so in a more troubling way than even psychoanalytic or deconstructive methods that criticize the texts of others. When a slip occurs there is no need to follow occult traces of repressed content or of marginal internal contradictions: its meaning is blatant. The slip signifies that its author is not an authority, because even that author's own discourse is out of control. This is true not only for writers who seek to achieve and believe in the possibility of mastery over language but also for writers who accept that mastery over language is tenuous at best, and perhaps not even desirable. Thus, the menace of the slip is not only that it reveals the artificiality of the hegemony of traditional structures of criticism and politics but that it undoes radical criticism as well. Because it rattles authority, it is best to avoid the discussion of slips entirely, especially since, as Freud points out:

> Now slips of the tongue are highly contagious, like the forgetting of names—a peculiar fact which Meringer and Mayer have noticed in the case of the latter. I cannot suggest any reason for this psychical contagiousness. (62)

To write about slips is to risk slipping, and even to mention them is to risk being infected by them. The slip is dangerous territory for the person whose identity, however theoretically well informed, is bound up in and dependent upon making convincing interpretations. For better or for worse, this is the structure of academic writing now, as it was in the early years of the century, when Freud piled up anecdotes relating to slips in academic writing and practice in *The Psychopathology of Everyday Life*. The unintentional letter, word, or phrase, however unavoidable, is undesirable, and everything possible is done to eliminate it, to stay aware and alert—not in order to increase one's knowledge of oneself but, rather, in order to avoid revealing one's ignorance.

I would like to suggest a reason for the contagiousness of slips. In an environment like an academic one, in which the emphasis is so heavily laid on having the right answer, in mastering the discourses, a great deal of tension is generated precisely in response to the need not to slip up. When someone finally does slip, the moment of release of control following that slip can make room for other slips to escape from the people who witnessed the first one. A slip may function as an unconscious invitation to self-revelation by dismantling, in one movement, the myth of unitary authority. It insists on the possibility of multiple discourses and of layered truths.

When Freud wanted to teach psychoanalysis he did not begin with jokes or dreams or a theory of personality: he started with slips. The first four of the *Introductory Lectures on Psychoanalysis* set out the whole of Freud's project in terms of parapraxes. I would like to transpose Freud's idea here to suggest that not only is the slip useful as an introductory concept in the teaching of psychoanalysis but that the slip itself is a way of teaching, a kind of pedagogy. As concept and as symptom, and then as object of analysis, the slip suggests a pedagogy that is not based on mastery, repression, or univocal authority. The slip teaches us to know that we do not know,[22] as well as to know that we do know things that we can only know we know if we surprise ourselves by emitting them in the presence of others.

At one point, in chapter 10 of *The Psychopathology of Everyday Life,* Freud mentions "another instructive error that put me to shame, an example of what might be called temporary ignorance" (220–21). This quotation summarizes the pedagogical utility of the slip. First, in terms of parapraxis, an error can only occur when one knows better—that is, one cannot stray from a path that one has not at some point been on. A parapraxis, then, uses error to bring previously unacknowledged information to light. Its instructiveness is related to its ability to put its author to shame—not in that it necessarily humiliates but, rather, in that it reveals the author's ignorance and hidden knowledge to someone else. Parapractic learning takes place in community. As a pedagogical tool, parapraxis works only if it is shared; this sharing could be conceived of as participating in shame, but only if it is shameful to expose, admit, and analyze the clumsy seams in one's authoritative discourse. If it is used as an occasion for shaming, then the slip's meaning can be revealed as a way of maintaining power over its author. But, if it is taken, instead, to be a manifestation of previously ignored knowledge, and a function of psychic and intellectual spontaneity, then it can be contagiously instructive.

Perhaps Faust's downfall was that he wanted knowledge but was unwilling to learn—that is, to expose the structures upholding his mastery to another in the process of questioning. The epigraph that

Freud uses for *The Psychopathology of Everyday Life* comes from one of Faust's monologues. I chose to start this essay with the *dialogue* that immediately follows what Freud quoted, when Faust turns outward, finally, to ask—even if in dread—"Is someone there?" and is greeted with Worry's response: "The question calls for Yes." *Faust,* a text whose hero, like all the heroes of traditional narrative[23] (and of criticism), can only exist by traversing an objectified and idealized femininity, is undone by a discourse, neither question nor answer, proceeding from a gendered position that exceeds the Faustian epistemology. In *Faust* this gendered position is named Worry, *Sorge,* and indicates the point at which authority slips. *Sorge,* as undominated femininity that slips in and undoes the Western mastermind, has a long tradition in philosophy, stretching from Goethe, through Freud and Heidegger, to Derrida.

The bodies of woman, text, and foreign tongue all serve as space in which discourses of mastery are enacted, and this is true, too, in *The Psychopathology of Everyday Life,* in which the slip is theorized and narrated through these categories. But, as in Freud's borrowed epigraph, which has a slip at its origin, the very narration of the slip, like the narration of woman, tends to cause the discourse that initially objectified it to slip itself. The Faustian monologue that depends for its authority on omniscience and domination gives way in this point of contact with another discourse that answers it, not to destroy but, instead, to reinvent. The answer-question posed by the feminine *Spuk* does not, in the poem, annihilate Faust. In dialogue with him it does alter his approach to knowledge, to what he knows and what he does not want to know. Ultimately, it brings his master narrative to a close and suggests another way of thinking. "The question calls for Yes [Die Frage fordert Ja]"—a question that demands affirmation of itself as *question* is worrysome, and for good reason, to the Faustian mind. It shows where that mind has limited itself.

My position in reference to *The Psychopathology of Everyday Life* has something in common with that of Worry in relationship to Faust. In dialogue with Freud's text, and borrowing from its vocabulary, I want to affirm my questions as a *Spuk* in the man's house of interpretation—as a questioning subject, gendered female but not contained by the patriarchal definitions of her identity and discourse. If Faust's monologue introduces *The Psychopathology of Everyday Life,* then let this study begin with a sister *Spuk* affirming my questions for Freud.

2

Someone Else

The second chapter of *The Psychopathology of Everyday Life*, "The Forgetting of Foreign Words," condenses and focuses a number of the
questions that I wish to pose with that text. It and the first chapter are
the only two to survive almost entirely unchanged from the first version of the book in 1901;[1] as such, they represent unrevised examples
of Freud's writing on slips and are the primordial public interpretations of them.[2] The reason why I am starting with the second chapter
rather than the first is that it unites the categories of woman, writing,
and foreign tongue in a more obvious way than does the "Signorelli"
example from the first chapter. There Freud literally sketches out in a
diagram a theory of the operation of parapraxis, which is then based
on his inability to remember the name of a painter. The first chapter
privileges image over text; for example, although words appear in
Freud's diagram, they float unlinked by conventional syntax (5). As
an introduction to his diagram, Freud says that the names that arose
as substitutions for Signorelli "have been treated in this process like
the pictograms in a sentence which has had to be converted into a
picture-puzzle (or rebus)" (5). The visual image of Signorelli's murals
of "The Four Last Things" in the Orvieto cathedral provokes a visual
attempt at an explanation of the forgetting of the painter's name, but
this diagram is even less effective than Freud's explanation in prose
(which itself is not the most lucid one he ever wrote). Perhaps the
relative expository inefficacy of the Signorelli chapter is the reason
why it, of all the examples in *The Psychopathology of Everyday Life*, is the
one that has interested critics most; it is the least threatening because
it is the least textualized and, thus, the least likely to be contagious to
other writing. Nevertheless, it lays out a number of themes that persist
throughout *The Psychopathology of Everyday Life*: the relationship between foreign words and prohibited sexuality; the location of narra-

tives about slips in foreign countries, where they occur in dialogues between traveling men; difficulties in identifying and identifying with canonical figures of Western culture. These currents, which appear for the first time in "The Forgetting of Proper Names" in reference to visual images, are more fully developed in terms of written texts in chapter 2, "The Forgetting of Foreign Words," and succeeding chapters.

The second chapter repeats the context of the first. Like it, the second chapter provides only one example of a slip. Both chapters are narrated in the context of a dialogue between Freud and another man during a holiday trip, and both depend upon Italian geography and Italian languages for their stimuli. But the slip in the second chapter is based on a written text rather than on a painting, and both the slip and its interpretation are constituted verbally rather than visually. Putting the slip into narrative in the second chapter sets the anecdotal pattern that will continue for the rest of the book; it also establishes the slip as written entity and privileges language as a determinant in the making and unraveling of slips.

The second chapter begins:

> The current vocabulary of our own language, when it is confined to the range of normal usage, seems to be protected against forgetting. With the vocabulary of a foreign language it is notoriously otherwise. (8)

Both here and in the first chapter the slip is narrated by means of the foreign—it takes place in foreign languages, on foreign soil, during conversations between men who are speaking their native languages but who need to use a foreign language *with and in* their native discourse in order to express, or repress, something for which the native tongue alone does not suffice.

> Last summer—it was once again on a holiday trip—I renewed my acquaintance with a certain young man of academic background. I soon found that he was familiar with some of my psychological publications. (8–9)

Two men of the same social class are traveling for the holidays; one is younger than the other, but they share an "academic background," that is, they have read and mastered the same canonical texts. They share a common discourse, and that discourse will determine the outcome of the interpretations produced by their conversation. The dialogue narrated by Freud is one between members of the same privileged group. But the privileges of class, sex, and education are not the only defining factors. The slip takes place while the two are talking "about the social status of the race to which we both belonged"; Freud's traveling companion is, like Freud, a Jew. The younger man gives "vent to a regret that his generation was doomed (as he expressed it) to atrophy, and could not develop its talents or satisfy its needs." Anti-Semitism was a serious obstacle to academic and professional advancement in Freud's Austria, both early in the century and later.[3] The friend wants to punctuate his "speech of impassioned fervour" against this state of affairs with a line from the *Aeneid*, in which Dido calls upon her descendants to take revenge upon Aeneas and his descendants. But at this point the friend goes silent; he cannot get the quotation right, so he rearranges the words:

Exoriar(e) ex nostris ossibus ultor.

[Let there arise from our bones an avenger.]

Apparently, Freud is not above shaming his friend for his error, because he quotes the young man as saying,

Please don't look so scornful: you seem as if you were gloating over my embarrassment. Why not help me? There's something missing in the line; how does the whole thing really go?

After pointing out the friend's frustration, Freud gives him the correct version of the quotation:

Exoriare ALIQUIS nostris ex ossibus ultor.

[Let SOMEONE arise from our bones as an avenger.]

The friend feels stupid at having forgotten the word, but he also knows that Freud claims "that one never forgets a thing without some reason" and says that he "should be very curious to learn how I came to forget the indefinite pronoun *'aliquis'* in this case." His attitude before his slip is instructive. It is customarily unpleasant for people of academic background to have to admit a lack of mastery over a classic text. But in this instance the man who slips is willing to learn[4] how it happened. To achieve this, Freud tells him to say, "*candidly* and *uncritically*," whatever comes into his mind in regard to the slip. This insistence upon free association begins the dialogue, itself represented as uninterrupted by critical remarks imposed from without, that recounts the analysis of the slip.

First, the friend divides *aliquis* into two words, *a* and *liquis*. Then he thinks of *reliquien* (relics), liquifying, fluidity, and fluid, followed by allusions to Saint Augustine and Saint Januarius (whom Freud calls calendar saints) and, finally, of the miracle of the annual liquefaction of Januarius' blood at Naples. This comes with a reference to the French occupation of that city, when the liquefaction was delayed until a general insistently hoped to the local priest that it would occur as soon as possible, which it did. At this point the man stalls in his associations but, when pressed by Freud, says,

> "Well then, I've suddenly thought of a lady from whom I might easily hear a piece of news that might be very awkward for both of us."
>
> "That her periods have stopped?"
>
> "How could you guess that?"
>
> "That's not difficult any longer; you've prepared the way sufficiently. Think of *the calendar saints, the blood that starts to flow on a particular day, the disturbance when the event fails to take place, the open threats that the miracle must be vouchsafed, or else. . . .* In fact you've made use of the miracle of St. Januarius to manufacture a brilliant allusion to women's periods." (11)

This is a conversation between two bourgeois men who are both inside (by virtue of their academic backgrounds) and outside (because of their Jewishness) their society's hegemony. While they are traveling for pleasure, they enact both a mastery over and a failure to dominate a classic text and then construct a scene that interprets that mastery and failure in terms of the female and the foreign. Men who travel together produce a certain kind of discourse—I am thinking of the

"farmer's daughter" jokes that were, not long ago, the staple of traveling salesmen. Exchanging stories about women from other geographical areas is something that Freud and his friend, traveling salesmen,
and soldiers have in common. Men who travel together through foreign lands tend to link their experience of the land with their experience of the women who live in it; both the land and the women are
spaces in which the men may take pleasure. When they discuss the
land and the women that they have enjoyed, the men are brought into
closer contact with each other. Foreign women and foreign lands serve
as exchange objects between traveling men, and discourse about them
reinforces the homosocial bond.

What I have just explained describes the standard patriarchal politics of travel narrative: the bond holding together a group of dominant
males is strengthened by the exchange of a specialized and closed
discourse about foreign women and feminized foreign lands.[5] But,
because of the question of anti-Semitism, in the *aliquis* anecdote the
situation is slightly more complicated. Regardless of the degree of the
assimilation of bourgeois European Jews in the first third of the twentieth century, there was an insistence by the Christian majority on con-
structing *the* "Jew" as a feminized, foreign other. The "Jew" was placed
on the same side of structures of binary opposition as "woman" and
the "foreign"; like them, the "Jew" was seen as erotically uncontrollable, mendacious, scheming, mysterious, not willing or able to uphold
the values of, and thus a threat to, Christian European civilization. But
the idea of the "Jew" was even more menacing than that of woman
and the foreign because, unlike the latter two terms, which remained
strictly within the limits imposed upon them, the "Jew" slipped between binarized concepts and thus threatened the discourse and definitions of established power. The "Jew" was constructed not only as
passionate but as learned and rational. The "Jew" was "foreign" but
excelled at the highest levels of European art and the professions.
Because it is both here and there, at home and foreign, the idea of the
"Jew" breaks down the rigidity of the boundaries that define the discourses of power.

For these reasons it is important to note the context in which the
slip in the *aliquis* example occurs:

The speaker had been deploring the fact that the present generation of his people was deprived of its full rights; a new generation,

he prophesied like Dido, would inflict vengeance on the oppressors. (14)

The problem of anti-Semitism and the misquotation of an ultracanonical text coincide in this conversation. Both the use of the canonical text and the slip itself are highly politicized; the friend counters a form of political oppression (anti-Semitism) with the citation of a text that has a very high cultural value in the oppressor's system. He is turning its own texts of power (over which he has mastery) back on it. The *Aeneid* is, in part, the story of the foundation of an empire; it glorifies and justifies the dominion of one nation over others and may be read as a literary enfranchisement of hegemony. The friend's reliance upon the quotation of the *Aeneid* as a function of political rhetoric poses the question of what it means for a despised other to cite a text that has helped to contruct oppression back at the oppressor. This question is at least partially explored in the engagement with psychoanalytic method that follows the representation of political desire (in the quotation) and its frustration (in the slip). Freud continues:

> He had in this way expressed his wish for descendants. At this moment a contrary thought intruded. "Have you really so keen a wish for descendants? That is not so. How embarrassed you would be if you were to get news just now that you were to expect descendants from the quarter you know of. No: no descendants—however much we need them for vengeance." (14)

The intensity of the friend's feelings makes it clear that he really does want some kind of vengeance against his oppressors; he wants someone (*aliquis*) to rise up from his failure and avenge the injustice done to him. To cite a master text back at the masters is to tell them that the seeds of their own fall are already present in the texts that they use to justify their dominion. But this use of the master's texts can be problematic for a radical reinterpreter of those texts. I will not go as far as Audre Lorde, who writes that "the master's tools will never dismantle the master's house,"[6] because I think that an engagement with and rereading of the master's texts can have a revolutionary effect on the way that culture is constructed. But I do think that the encounter with those texts will test the depths of a critic's radical commitment and show where it is weak or co-opted.

Freud's friend stumbles over his citation of Virgil and cannot help but delete a crucial part of it: *aliquis*, the pronoun that indicates the unknown someone else, whose job it will be to achieve the justice left undone in the present. The friend wants someone to avenge him, but the slip marks the degree to which he is unwilling to upset another hegemonic social structure in order to attain his goal; the announcement of the imminent birth of a descendant, he says, "would be very awkward" (11). Its awkwardness stems from the fact that it would further disrupt the young man's professional ambitions, and be a source of social shame, if he were discovered to have fathered an illegitimate child. As much as he may want descendants who can put right the wrongs done to him because of anti-Semitism, he is still heavily invested in other values of the dominant culture and unwilling to go all out against them: any descendants that he may have must participate in existing forms of legitimacy. It is interesting that this resistance to his own radical project (attacking and dismantling an oppressive system by means of its own texts) should be grounded or located in the realm of paternity. His allegiance to patriarchy undoes him. Because the friend cannot give up the privileges of enfranchised fatherhood—that is, because of his identification with the rule of the father—his political desire to combat anti-Semitism frustrates itself. The slip in his citation of Virgil shows where his political commitment slips; if respectability (i.e., the approval of the dominant society) matters more than vengeance, or the reordering of social categories, then very little can be achieved. In the case of Freud's young friend, and in radical criticisms in general, the slip is thus evidence of an undertow of orthodoxy and accommodation. It shows how perilous it can be to use hegemonic texts to critique hegemony; canonized readings of the texts of power are so strong that they can wreak havoc with what one wants to say with or against them. It is hard to borrow Dido's words without borrowing her defeat and self-destruction as well.

Freud does not tell the reader what happened to the friend or to his Italian lover. The text does not say whether the friend's desire for vengeance was finally thwarted or fulfilled; Freud has the last word in the interpretive dialogue, and the friend disappears from the narrative. The pedagogical intent of the dialogue from Freud's point of view seems to be twofold: to prove to his friend that the slip has meaning and to prove that meaning to the reader as well. Both its personal and its political implications for the friend drop out of the text in favor of the assertion of the mastery of Freud's method. Similarly, the issue of anti-Semitism, which was the catalyst for the quotation and for the slip, is set aside, because the very mention of anti-Semitism, as an emblem of its real historical influence and its role in frustrating the careers of talented men, threatens the positive reception of Freud's theories and discoveries.

The goal of this pedagogical dialogue is not to address political problems but, rather, is merely to prove that the teacher knows more than the student. The dialogue reproduces existing hierarchies and depoliticizes what started out as a political conversation. The analytic method illustrated in the *aliquis* chapter does not show how an analysand (or a radical discourse) can learn from its own points of slippage; it only seeks to prove its own legitimacy by showing that a discourse has slipped, and for what reason. At this point Freud is too interested in asserting the correctness of his own answer to be able to help the friend to learn anything about himself. In order to be politically effective, a radical criticism must disrupt the traditional hierarchy that privileges answer over question. Instead of what happens in Freud's version of the narrative, in which the answer seeks to fulfill and put an end to the question, it could be acknowledged that the answer and question exist in a symbiotic discursive relationship, that one does not have meaning without the other, and that a belief in an absolute mastery is the death of inquiry. The friend's first impulse when he sees Freud grimacing at his error is to ask for a correction that will put an end to his embarrassment. But it also shows him moving beyond shame to analysis:

> How stupid to forget a word like that! By the way, you claim that one never forgets a thing without some reason. I should be very curious to learn how I came to forget the indefinite pronoun *aliquis* in this case. (9)

The friend vacillates between the question and the answer, between wanting and not wanting to know. He is tending toward political engagement, but his own co-optation and Freud's displacement of the friend's questions in favor of his own answer make it possible for difficult but crucial matters—like anti-Semitism and the rupture of patriarchal rules—to disappear from the discussion. Correction can be used to put an end to dialogue.

Nevertheless, Freud's strategy does have political implications; it suggests that, if radical discourse slips—and, in so doing, shows where it is in league with orthodoxy—so might the discourses of power slip and thereby indicate where they can be taken apart. For example, Freud's narrative avoids analyzing a certain stumble in the friend's process of association, even while dutifully recording that it occurred:

> The people attach great importance to this miracle and get very excited if it's delayed, as happened once at a time when the French were occupying the town. So the general in command—or have I got it wrong? was it Garibaldi?—took the reverend gentleman aside and gave him to understand, with an unmistakable gesture to the soldiers posted outside, that he *hoped* a miracle would take place very soon. And in fact it did take place.... (10)

Freud quotes the friend's explanation of the miracle of Saint Januarius but does not comment on the confusion between Garibaldi (the father of Italian unification) and the alien French general. The point of this unanalyzed forgetfulness is that it indicates the elasticity of the boundaries between opposing factions in a political conflict and the difficulty of distinguishing between the categories "ally" and "enemy," between home and the foreign. The absence of an analysis of this point of confusion—again of a foreign name (that of the French general)—is symptomatic of ambivalence about taking up a position in reference to a political and historical reality.

The stumble around the name of the general does not fit in with Freud's answer to the friend's slip, and so it is left outside the analysis. But because it is an allusion to war and to the relationship between religion and political conflict, and, finally, an indication of an inability to decide whose side one is on, it marks the return of the displaced issue of anti-Semitism. Not being able to distinguish between Garibaldi and a French general not only puts into doubt who is on my side but also puts into question whose side *I* am on. Like bourgeois, male members of despised ethnic or religious groups, "persons of academic background" who are members of oppressed groups living in the late twentieth century find themselves both "here" and "there," on both sides of matters of privilege and oppression. A refusal to choose sides may be a strategic move to avoid the limitations imposed by adherence to unnecessary oppositions, or it may be a passive form of accommodation to oppressive structures. In either case, or in others that may arise, such a radical critic may find herself in a situation like that of Freud's friend, in which the demands of respectability (or of one's profession) conflict with legitimate and urgent political desires; the result is a discourse that undermines itself.

One way through this difficulty is to analyze one's own points of slippage. As I have explained, the young friend shows some will to do this, and Freud indicates a way, or method, that still could work today. But there is a further caution to be taken from the *aliquis* example and its evasion of the problem of anti-Semitism. The reason that the narrative *cannot* develop a discourse against anti-Semitism is that its analytic scene, like the friend's solution to his dilemma over descendants, remains ensconced in patriarchal modes. The problem with this scene is that, on multiple levels, the body of a woman is made to serve as the ground for "academic" dialogue. The desires to keep mastery over paternity, of a child or of a theory, make it impossible for Freud and his friend to analyze the structures of domination that make not only racism (as anti-Semitism) but also sexism possible. The need to retain patriarchal dominance here makes it impossible to work against racism. Two men talking together would rather sacrifice themselves than sacrifice their dominance over woman, and thus, at least in terms of politics, their discourse becomes reactionary. A narrative that begins by being about anti-Semitism turns into a story of a vacation fling that went wrong; it also proves the persistence of the connection between racism and sexism and makes clear yet again that it is not possible to work against the former without combating the latter.

In this anecdote sexism derails discourse against racism. Racism derives its power from the enfranchisement of the belief that difference is a measure of inferiority: that which is like me is superior; that which is unlike me is inferior. Sexism reproduces the same structures, only along lines of gender rather than of ethnicity. In the *aliquis* anecdote the foreign, in terms of linguistic, geographical, ethnic, and sexual categories, becomes the locus of difference. The friend, in his ambivalent wish for descendants, and his repressed knowledge that they might come from a foreign source, intuits the fact that his fate is bound up with that of someone who is different from him, but he cannot go so far as to embrace that knowledge as something not foreign to him. If the project of radical politics can be defined as work that intends to replace dominance with mutuality, then it must confront structures of dominance and exploitation where they live—and with some frequency, and not just in institutional or academic practice, they live at home with us, not somewhere else.

The problem for members of groups that are oppressed to greater or lesser degrees is that, because our own oppression is foregrounded in our experience, it is easy not to see how it is connected to other people's and, further, how we, in the elaborate scheme of what seems to be survival's pecking order, accommodate ourselves to our own and other people's oppression. The *aliquis* example shows how two professional Jewish men maintain some privilege in the face of virulent anti-Semitism by sticking to the rules of the same public morality that would call them infanticidal.[7] The situation might be updated to that of two lesbian professionals, for example, who pay a poor woman discount rates to do their child care and who do not or have conveniently forgotten to realize that the classist and racist pattern that they are repeating is part of the same one that would challenge their right, as gay parents, to the custody of their own children. Or an African-American intellectual expresses anti-Semitic opinions, in the process eliding the fact that dark-skinned people were gassed next to Jews in Nazi camps. A group of gay men fight for better AIDS research but do not educate themselves about feminism because they fail to realize that misogyny is at the root of homophobia. What these not at all random examples[8]—they hit me where I live—hope to indicate is that the equivocal privileges of class, profession, or race held by people who are neither here nor there—that is, people of despised groups who have achieved or been granted some of the privileges of power— tend to be maintained by the subjection of an even less powerful, foreign, and feminine or feminized other.

This foreign other, by projection, becomes a repository for the internal difference that the "in" person of an "out" group must displace in order to keep his or her privilege. It is possible to use both the male and the female pronouns here because, regardless of sexual orientation, the somewhat oppressed person's identification and political position in reference to the even more oppressed foreign is always that of masculine to feminine, whether that femininity is incarnated as language, text, or body. The opposition masculine-feminine is the cornerstone from which relationships of social and political power are defined and constructed. I develop this notion, in terms of a Freudian definition of the words *masculine* and *feminine,* from Monique Wittig's comments in the essay "On the Social Contract" :

> Aristotle was much more cynical when he stated in *The Politics* that things *must be:* "The first point is that those which are ineffective without each other *must be* united in a pair. For example, the union of male and female" (emphasis added). Notice that this point of the necessity of heterosexuality is the first point of *The Politics.* And notice also that the second example of "those . . . which *must be* united as a pair" is found in "the combination of ruler and ruled." From that time on, male and female, the heterosexual relationship, has been the parameter of all hierarchical relations. It is almost useless to underline that it is only the dominated members of the pair that are "ineffective" by themselves. For "ruler" and "male" go very well without their counterpart.[9]

I am not sure that Wittig here refers necessarily to all possible sexual practices between biologically male and female people; I think, rather, that her emphasis is on the construction of sexual difference in terms of the dominance of male over female, which is why I use the terms *masculine* and *feminine* in my formulation. Also, Wittig is not the first to trace the origins of domination to the oppression of the female by the male, but I think that her example is useful because it is grounded on a primordial text of Western law, Aristotle's *Politics.* This grounding makes explicit the connections between sexism and a political order founded upon dominance.

Within this system Freud's young friend needs to give expression to political feeling but is unwilling to sacrifice male privilege in order to achieve the goal his outrage seeks. His ambivalence leads him to use the words of another—foreign words, in that they are Latin and belong to Virgil and Dido. These foreign words, by way of the slip, lead to foreign places and to prohibited desire—that is, desire that threatens to break through the same structures of accommodation that led to the use of the foreign tongue in the first place. This irrepressible desire returns to menace the friend's ties to patriarchy at the same place where his allegiance to respectability undercuts his political project. In *The Psychopathology of Everyday Life* the slip marks not only the undertow of currents that contradict the conscious intent of a discourse but also indicates where structures of domination ordered specifically by gender may be taken apart.

N before M, or Learning the Alphabet from a Woman

Prohibited desire may be defined as desire that undoes patriarchy. In the case of Freud's friend desire for the Italian woman is not prohibited, because to have amorous adventures in foreign parts with foreign females is part of the colonizing enterprises of patriarchy. On the other hand, to desire to have children by this woman, outside the accepted social structures, and, further, to wish that these children would avenge the wrongs perpetrated upon their father because of the ways that he cannot fit in with dominant social norms, is prohibited. To acknowledge illegitimate children is to break the power of the name of the father. I have tried to show how the friend's ambivalence about being on both sides of respectability and prohibition leads him to verbalize his dilemma by the use of a foreign language. The idea is that repression is what leads to the use of the foreign language but, then, that the foreign language makes possible a slip that redirects discourse from repression to expression. The use of the foreign tongue is originally meant to stave off prohibited desire, but it ends up abetting it. In part this is because to speak a foreign tongue inevitably produces some kind of feminine identification in its speaker. If the speaker's native tongue is one that is in a position of cultural dominance relative to the foreign tongue being spoken, then he yields linguistic dominance during the time that he uses the foreign tongue, *even if* he is using it for colonizing purposes. To speak the language of the "weak" is self-feminizing and perverse in the sense of old-fashioned etiologies of homosexuality, which saw the homosexual as a man who made himself womanly in respect to other men. (This may be why the teaching of languages other than English is seen as so insidious by linguistic nationalists in the United States.) If the speaker's native tongue is in a position of cultural inferiority to the foreign tongue being spoken, that speaker, too, feminizes himself, because to accede to the grammar of the powerful is to submit, and to submit is feminine.

In this scheme language begins to function as a series of Oedipus complexes, which, instead of determining sexuality, determine positions in political hierarchies. Because of this, women who speak as feminists in patriarchal systems are necessarily seen as speaking foreign languages and only confirm their own foreignness (as femininity). I should clarify here by stating that I am referring to what might be called public speaking, or discourse, that which takes place in the political and intellectual marketplace. It is still true that a woman who, as a feminist authority, makes her words public, whether in her native or a foreign tongue, is rare. Most feminist discourses are foreign languages as far as public speaking is concerned, and women who print their words in public find few interlocutors unless they write or talk like the man. In a recent interview Susie Bright, a lesbian cultural analyst, told the commentarist Camille Paglia that plenty of feminists were writing things of import that Paglia had no idea about. Paglia's response was, "But they're not making any impact!"[1]—that is, they had not, like Paglia, been on "Donahue" and "Geraldo" and had not sold their books to Vintage. This is not because feminists have no language or because they have had no access to it or even because what they are saying is dull or trite or politically correct. It is because the dominant society cannot understand what we are saying, because it has not learned the languages of feminism, and it has not learned those languages, because to learn them would put it in the uncomfortable position of Freud's friend, that is, one of challenging its own values. In these terms I find the quest for an *écriture féminine*, a specific form of women's writing, somewhat beside the point. Feminists are already writing and publishing. What is necessary is listeners and readers who have trained themselves to understand these already published words and to enter into a dialogue with them. Of course, to do this is to risk the feminization that I allude to earlier.

Fortunately, dominance is built on a fiction and, as a text, is subject to analysis. Because it is founded in language, it has seams, places where it can be taken apart and reconstituted, and sometimes it shows them. The political utility of being both inside and outside structures of power is that one can work on the seams from both sides, with some hope that meanings will pass through in both directions and effect some structural change. The seam and the slip have something in common; in English they both can be read as alluding to clothing. Specifically, a slip is a woman's undergarment, and, not coincidentally, it is an undergarment that breaks down the distinction between underwear and outerwear. To wear a slip is not to be fully dressed, but it is not to be in a complete state of undress either. A woman in a slip is neither public nor private and, thus (between those overdefined boundaries), may be curiously comfortable. But the slip is not seamless; despite its elasticity, it is part of the preparations for putting on or taking off that specifically feminine garment, the skirt. The slip is a stage in the process of putting on or taking off femininity, and here the meaning of the garment and the slip as parapraxis meet. A woman who knows the slip's seams, that is, where and how it is put together and how it can be taken apart, can use that knowledge to her own advantage. But a man who finds himself in a slip, especially if he is in the company of other men who are not, is in trouble. If he is in a slip, it is because he put it on, as foreign as that may seem to him. To slip is to miss mastery, to lose control, and to reveal the places where one coincides with or identifies with what has been traditionally defined as the feminine. For this reason it should not be surprising to discover that, in *The Psychopathology of Everyday Life,* so many examples of slips involving foreign words and phrases should involve bodies of women that exceed patriarchal control.[2]

In the particular case of the *aliquis* anecdote it is the female bodily function of menstruation that invades and disrupts the conversation between men. The Italian woman's periods have stopped. That the friend knows this is an indication that, although their liaison is over, he and the woman are still in communication. Her body is still influencing his language. Evidently, the possibility of conception that her stopped periods indicate was not planned by the couple. The man does not want the woman to have become pregnant, but she may have, anyway. Her body is communicating messages by witholding the fluid—menstrual blood—that would signify that it would not disrupt the man's life. This foreign woman had been scripted as part of an adventure in traveling, but she was not to be more, not to become legally inscribed, as a wife or mother, in the man's life. Nevertheless, her female body does not participate in the contracts of the male narrative; it has an insistent story of its own to tell. Because of this other discourse and its potential ramifications, the men's conversation is interrupted and redirected.

Women's sexuality and reproduction exceed the rules of patriarchal narrative. The presence or lack of menstrual blood in this example shows the lack of fluency, in the sense of control over a language, that men may demonstrate when it comes to the significations produced by the female body. Menstrual blood is worse than the subjunctive, the ablative absolute, verbs of direction, the optative—pick your worst grammatical nightmare. It is unpronouncable, unrepeatable, impossible to master—but not because it is difficult or irrational. The problem posed by menstrual blood or its absence is the problem of a gender whose etymology is the female body, but which is not defined by, or exceeds the definitions of, patriarchy. Because it exceeds the dictionary, it trips up the grammar.

The first association that the friend has after he decides to analyze his forgetfulness is "the ridiculous notion of dividing the word up like this: *a* and *liquis* (9)." The notion (*Einfall,* or association) is ridiculous because the form is ungrammatical, meaningless according to the rules of Latin. Only someone capable of *mis*understanding Latin can make any sense of it: to such a person it might mean "from or by means of liquid or liquidity," or at any rate having to do somehow with liquid or the lack of it. It is a bad and barbaric pun that signifies the neither present nor absent menstrual blood.[3] The signification of the menstrual blood only becomes a problem for the man because he has risked contact with the female body. He can only get what he wants (pleasure or descendants, or both) if he makes that contact. But to do so is to expose himself to the (for him) unmanageable foreign language of the feminine. Sometimes this contact may result in an outcome that serves patriarchy; other times it will not. When it does not, it will interrupt the discourse of dominance and cause it to change. This is evident in the immediate results of the initial associations. After the friend says "*a* and *liquis,*" Freud asks him, "What does that mean?" The friend answers, "I don't know." Freud asks him to continue, and the friend says:

"What comes next is *Reliquien* [relics], *liquefying, fluidity, fluid.* Have you discovered anything so far?"

"No, not by any means yet. But go on." (9)

Both the friend and Freud confess ignorance before the ungrammatical notions. The men cannot make meaning from them, because they thwart authoritative quotation and grammatical solutions and insist, instead, upon further, tentative dialogue, interdependent questions and responses, and a process of learning together. Mastery will reassert itself in Freud's narration of the story, but it is not the informing catalyst for the event's meaning. One might try to use the dialogue produced by psychoanalytic method to obtain mastery over someone else, but it would seem that one does so at one's own peril, because the ungrammatical will always exceed and displace the interpretive powers of mastery.

I do not wish to suggest by this that the female body as language is ungrammatical or irrational or any of the other adjectives traditionally used to degrade its meanings. What I am trying to say is that the female body can make the discourses of patriarchy and masculinity ungrammatical, that is, can cause them to err. To err, to wander off the approved path, is, literally, deviant: that which, by definition, does not follow the rules. The desire not to slip is the desire to stay within the rules; fear of slipping is the fear of losing one's way. But to slip is merely to find another way, or to find oneself on a path that one did not know one was already on. When a person refuses to admit having made a slip, Freudian theory says it is because the slip contains information that the person would consciously prefer to repress. But the fact that the slip has made other information apparent indicates that the person has already erred, somewhere, and, rather than having lost the one and only way, is traveling two ways simultaneously. The alternative meaning of the slip is an argument for psychic richness and flexibility. But it is terrifying because it does not come of conscious choice, challenges unitary authority, and breaks down discourses of univocal power. To accept the possibility of slipping, to slip, and to explore the slip's meanings is to change epistemologies. It allows for the possibility of knowing and not knowing simultaneously. This position can make for some anxiety. It is how a woman feels when her menstrual period has not come on time and she thinks she might be pregnant, or not.

Is it possible that making a Freudian slip makes a man feel pregnant with unwelcome meanings? Feminized and oversignifying? Three other anecdotes in *The Psychopathology of Everyday Life* might amplify these questions. They come from the chapter "Childhood and

Screen Memories" (chap. 4), which appeared for the first time in the second (1907) edition of the book, and are the only anecdotes that appear in that chapter. Freud included information on screen memories in *The Psychopathology of Everyday Life* because both screen memories and the forgetting of names "have to do with mistakes in remembering: what the memory reproduces is not what it should correctly have reproduced, but something else as a substitute" (45).

Two of the three screen memories analyzed in the chapter have to do directly with a little boy's reaction to his mother's being with child; the third is less explicitly about a mother's pregnancy but, nevertheless, helps explain the way that slips narrate themselves over the semiotic field of a woman's body. None of the three examples in the chapter on screen memories deals with the responses of girl children to their mothers' pregnancies. I am explicating the representation of the reactions of boy children in *The Psychopathology of Everyday Life* as a step toward a feminist psychoanalysis of Freudian psychoanalysis. (This book itself might be read as one grown girl child's response to this and other issues raised by *The Psychopathology of Everyday Life.*) The order in which I will consider the anecdotes is the reverse of that in which they are presented in Freud's narration; I will start with the last and end with the first because that order will help show the connotative coherence of the three anecdotes.

The last anecdote in the chapter is an autobiographical one that Freud dates to before he turned three years old:

> I saw myself standing in front of a cupboard [Kasten] demanding something and screaming, while my half-brother, my senior by twenty years, held it open. Then suddenly my mother, looking beautiful and slim, walked into the room, as if she had come in from the street. (50)

His briefest explanation of the episode is that he

> had missed his mother, and had come to suspect that she was shut up in this wardrobe or cupboard; and it was for this reason that I was demanding that my brother should open the cupboard. When he did what I asked and I had made certain that my mother was not in the cupboard, I began to scream. This is the moment

that my memory has held fast; and it was followed at once by the appearance of my mother, which allayed my anxiety or longing.

The reason he thought that his brother might have put his mother in the cupboard [Kasten] is that this same brother had caused a theiving nurse of little Freud's to be locked up, or "boxed up" (eingekastelt) (51); the child Freud was afraid that the brother had boxed his mother up in a cupboard, too. The importance of the slimness of the mother is that "it had just been restored to her"; she had just given birth to a child, a sister two and a half years younger than Freud. The little boy did not want any further additions to the family to emerge from his mother's inside, whose meaning he had conflated with *cupboard.* (51 n. 2).

The child prefers his mother slender; largeness is ugly because it rekindles the memory of a pregnant mother and a new sibling, who will displace the primacy of the older child. The mother's pregnancy destroys the child's belief that he is all that matters to her and that she is his alone. The father is noticeably absent from this narration; it is the brother who is thought to have "had in some way introduced the recently born baby into his mother's inside" (51 n. 2). But oedipal and sibling rivalry are developments of the fundamental problem, which is, even for the two-and-a-half-year-old, not so much that his own but, rather, that his mother's body contradicts the child's wishes and is an unpredictable and uncontrollable producer of excessive meanings that impact upon the child's position in and ways of understanding his world. Furthermore, the surprises that her body produces are invisible until, with little or no warning, they burst onto the scene. The child cannot ever master them. They appear of their own accord. (And the threat of the pregnant mother persists—how long? Even until the grown child receives some unhoped-for news from a former girl-friend?) The father or other male figure who is supposed to have introduced the baby into the mother is incidental, at least at this point. The problem is specifically the mother's body and its (for the boy child) excessiveness.

The chapter on screen memories also presents two ways that older male children, those who have already embarked on their oedipal journeys, might deal with the anxieties provoked by the mother's body. In the second of the three anecdotes Freud tells of a man of forty, the eldest of nine children, who maintained that he never noticed any of his mother's pregnancies. Finally, he remembered that

> at the age of eleven or twelve he had seen his mother hurriedly *unfasten* her skirt in front of the mirror. He now added of his own accord that she had come in from the street and had been overcome by unexpected labour pains. The unfastening [Aufbinden] of the skirt was a screen memory for the confinement [Entbindung]. We shall come across the use of "verbal bridges" of this kind in further cases. (49)

This man's reactions to his mother's pregnancies is an almost total repression of any knowledge of them; he cannot consciously see them and then replaces his sight of them with the sight of something else, much as a fetishist replaces his knowledge of his mother's castration with a fetish meant to take the place of her "missing" penis. The attention to the unfastening of the skirt in front of the mirror, in particular, has fetishistic overtones, but, instead of covering up the perception of a *lack* in the mother's body, it covers up the perception of an *excess*. The mother's bulging body pushes castration as lack aside but poses an analogous problem. If fetishism is founded upon the boy's idea that his mother has been castrated and that it can happen to him, too, then might the repression of the sight of a mother's pregnancy stem from the idea that, if it can happen to her, it can happen to me, too? When it is not complicated by the desire to have a female body and a baby by the father,[4] it is possible that the mother's pregnant body signifies castration *by its excess*. In this example her pregnancy causes the mother's body to exceed the clothing that it is supposed to fit inside; the constructions that cover it up and determine how and what it may signify in society come apart at the seams because of the pregnancy—thus, both excessiveness and lack become defining terms of femininity.

The fact that the mother unfastens her skirt hurriedly "in front of the mirror" adds a further dimension to the scene. If the mother is in front of the mirror, then she is not looking at her son; she is looking at herself. The mother looking at herself, and not at the son, sets up a system of gazes in which the son may not participate; her attention is withdrawn to something that is out of his sight. The demands of the labor pains utterly displace whatever needs or concerns the boy may have had at the moment, and this is true of either the moment of unfastening (Aufbinden) or actual confinement (Entbindung). Also, if the mother is in front of the mirror, then the boy cannot see himself in it; the mother's pregnancy with a younger sibling interrupts the pleasures of narcissism. It puts an end to the boy's fiction of his own priority.

A similar process is at work in the anecdote I will discuss last, which is the first in Freud's arrangement. It is of particular interest because it links questions of sexual difference with writing and reading:

> A man of twenty-four has preserved the following picture from his fifth year. He is sitting in the garden of a summer villa, on a small chair beside his aunt, who is trying to teach him the letters of the alphabet. He is in difficulties over the difference between *m* and *n* and he asks his aunt to tell him how to know one from the other. His aunt points out to him that the *m* has a whole piece more than the *n*—the third stroke. (48)

Freud explicitly links this memory to the boy's desire "to find out the difference between boys and girls" and to have this same aunt teach him; his final discovery is "that a boy, too, has a whole piece more than a girl." This anecdote traces the development of the fiction of the priority of the male. The first step in learning to record language in writing, and to read the written records of others, is to learn the alphabet. *M*, the letter of masculinity, precedes *n* in the order of the letters. But when the letter *m* is written, *n* precedes *it*. *N* is, inevitably, the first part of *m*, every time. In the act of writing, the existence of *m* derives from *n* and also depends upon it. The fact that *m* has "a whole piece more" than *n* cannot disturb *n*'s priority. The symbolic economy that privileges that which has a whole piece more over that which has a whole piece less is the same economy in which that which comes first (is born first) is better than that which comes after. But the relationship between *m* and *n* in terms of their construction and the mechanics of writing mangles the logic of a hegemony based on priority.

The presence of *n* in *m* also reorients the alphabet of gender. To continue with Freud's analogy, the standard notion that the male is superior to the female because of its whole piece more, and that the woman consequently envies that extra piece, is displaced in the relationship between the two letters. If (let us continue to learn the alphabet from a woman) every *m* contains an *n*, and yet *n* is different from and thus inferior to *m*, then *m* must do everything possible to negate its dependence upon, and descent from, *n*. N is the not-me that, I uncomfortably discover, is not only part of me but also essential to my being. The fear, then, is not so much of losing the whole piece more but, rather, of acknowledging that the *n* is present inside me all the time.

At the point at which the boy is learning the alphabet, he cannot distinguish between *m* and *n*. That is why he asks for help from his aunt. He wants his aunt to help him to recognize difference so that he can participate in written language. Thus, for him, the source of written language, the key to it, and the way of understanding it is intimately linked with the body of a woman that he desires: the aunt who teaches him to read and write by teaching him the difference between the letters is the same one from whom he would like to learn the difference between the sexes. In this example the body is textualized as a letter of the alphabet and transmuted into something to be written and read. Freud's interpretation of the screen memory theorizes gender difference as based on the anatomy of language, on the bare bones of it, the letters that make it up.

But language is as paradoxical as human anatomy is—the difference between *m* and *n* is less reassuring than it first appears to be, since, instead of distinguishing clearly between the two letters, it shows where they run together and how the one that claims superiority in fact always carries inside it a sign that it comes from that which it denies. Gender slips in Freud's theorizing of the Freudian slip; the feminine is always slipping into the masculine in *The Psychopathology of Everyday Life*, just as *n* twines in and out of *m*. The chapter on screen memories depends upon a constant building of theory on the narration of pregnancy as a sign of excessive meaning: first with Freud's disappearing mother; second, with the mother whose pregnancy obscures her son's view of himself in the mirror; and, finally, with the biologized letters of the alphabet, which show a boy how *m* comes out of *n*. In this regard *m* is the mark of an excessive *masculinity*, one that is capable of containing, or is impregnated with, unwanted feminine meanings that may slip out at any time—that is, a masculinity that is not reliably manly at all. In this chapter a theory built on boys' narrations of female bodies demonstrates the possibility and actuality of the presence of the foreign inside them and the men that they wish they had become.

This is what happens, too, back in the *aliquis* anecdote in chapter 2, in which Freud's friend "end[s] a speech of impassioned fervour with the well-known line of Virgil's in which the unhappy Dido commits to posterity her vengeance on Aeneas" (9). Because the friend cannot control the internal multiplicity of his lover, his own gender slips; he expresses himself with the words of a wronged woman, Dido, and feminizes himself. The words he is using are foreign, since they are in Latin, and feminine, because they are identified with the character Dido. He turns himself into the foreign woman abandoned by the traveling man and then finds himself unexpectedly full of unanticipated meanings; his whole process of slipping identifies him with the possibly pregnant Italian woman whom he left behind, and he becomes foreign to himself. What began as a rhetorical flourish in a political speech ends up as "a brilliant allusion to women's periods." Political and sexual ambivalences are played out over the body of a woman and narrated through the processes of menstruation and pregnancy. The woman is seen as foreign, but her femininity and foreignness become a mirror in which the man may notice his own otherness and signifying excess.

For this reason it will come as no surprise that the question of abortion plays a part in the theorizing of the slip, too. Near the end of their dialogue the friend asks:

> "And you really mean to say that it was this anxious expectation that made me unable to produce an unimportant word like *aliquis*?"
>
> "It seems to me undeniable. You need only recall the division you made into *a-liquis,* and your associations: *relics, liquefying, fluid.* St. Simon was *sacrificed as a child*—shall I go on and show how he comes in? You were led on to him by the subject of relics."
>
> "No, I'd much rather you didn't." (11)

The friend does not say whether he would want the Italian woman to have an abortion or not. All that he does is to stop dialogue relating to abortion. But the allusion to Saint Simon is interpreted by Freud as signaling at least some wish to eradicate any possibility of descendants from the liaison with the Italian woman. In the discourse of theory the woman's choice in the matter is irrelevant. Here and elsewhere the female body and the woman have no voice at all, and any signifying system ordered by their experience is absent. The woman's body exists only insofar as it can help the men to talk about each other. As many critics have noted, it would seem that this is still the structure of debates about abortion in the United States in the late twentieth century: at the levels of power in which legal and religious decisions are made, they are a way for men to interact passionately with one another over the bodies of women.

It is difficult but not impossible to find in Freud's writings indications that might point the way to a way of making theory (whether psychoanalytic, political, or literary) that does not so traduce the female body. One such example might appear in an earlier essay in which Freud published an example of another autobiographical memory, again from before his third birthday.[5] In this anecdote Freud reports being a little boy and, with another little boy, stealing a bunch of bright yellow flowers, which he thinks must have been dandelions, from a little girl. The little girl runs for consolation to a peasant woman, who has been talking in front of a cottage with a children's nurse, and receives from the peasant woman a big piece of black bread. Little Freud and his accomplice drop their flowers and run to get some bread, too. The woman gives them each a piece, "cut[ting] the loaf with a long knife." Freud analyzes this anecdote as a screen memory produced in adolescence, when he had a strong crush on a young woman from the same area, who wore a bright yellow dress. He realizes that to take her flowers is to *deflower* her, a wish on the part of the enamored boy. The bread is a reference to Freud's desire for different and easier career and life circumstances, which would have made it possible for him to stay in the country (the scene of the screen memory) and to marry the girl with the dandelion dress.

The presence of the boy cousin helping Freud to take away the girl's flowers—"'can you make any sense of the idea of being helped in deflowering someone? or of the peasant woman and the nurse in front of the cottage?' 'Not that I can see.'"(319)—is seen as not symbolically relevant to the analysis and, as such, a confirmation of the memory's genuineness. In terms of self-analysis, this setting aside of information may make sense, but, in terms of a psychoanalytic reading of the anecdote, it looks like an evasion. The two boys first take the girl's flowers for themselves and then throw them down in favor of a piece of the bread that the girl was eating. The fundamental fact of the anecdote is that, this time, the boys want what the *girl* has—first the flowers and then the bread. They take the flowers from her, even though each of them has a bunch and the field is full of them. When they see that the peasant woman has given her bread, they want that, too, but this time each is satisfied with his own piece; perhaps the presence of the long knife enforces that satisfaction. It is possible to read the anecdote as a fable of matriarchy, of a preoedipal stratum in Freud's development (the anecdote relates to Freud's "birthplace, and therefore date from [his] second and third years" [309]), in which the female body is the source and root of meaning. The first "birthplace" is the mother's body. And here the long knife does not castrate but, rather, resolves a conflict by transmuting a unitary, single piece of bread (the loaf) into enough pieces to provide for everyone's satisfaction. The female is the primary signifier, and so castration is irrelevant. In this fable lack has ceased to operate, and the knife, instead of mutilating, nurtures.

It is interesting, too, that no parent is present in the scene and no siblings; the oedipal is absent. Perhaps the memory might be read as an awareness on the part of the adult (forty-three-year-old) Freud of the existence of the preoedipal period, upon which he would touch tangentially but which he would never fully theorize. To Freud's perpetual regret his family was forced by financial problems to leave his birthplace for good when he was only three. Freud's adult memories of the journey from Freiberg through Breslau to Leipzig, where the family spent a year before moving on to Vienna, become crucial to his self-analysis; he invokes them, in particular, in letters to Fliess about his work on dissipating his intense "travel phobia." Ernest Jones reports that this fear, from which Freud suffered for twelve years, "turned out to be connected with the fear of losing his home (and ultimately his mother's breast)—a panic of starvation which must have been in its turn a reaction to some infantile greed."[6] The motivation for this first voyage away from home is the will of the father; because of his father's power, he was forced to leave his birthplace *and* the body of his mother. He says that he

never felt really comfortable in the town ... [and was] never free
from a longing for the beautiful woods near our home, in which
(as one of my memories from those days tells me) I used to run
off from my father, almost before I learned to walk. (312–13)

The birthplace is a place where it is possible to escape the rule of the
father and where the freedom of running is easier than walking.

The little Freud had no choice but to go where he was told to go,
but it is notable that the adult writer so strongly senses that having
left makes it feel impossible to go back. The privileges of the postoedi-
pal make it impossible for most people to sustain a knowledge of
home simultaneously with a knowledge of the way stations on the
voyage out. Because survival in reality is so dependent upon going
with the father, the legal residence, paradoxically, becomes where he
is, and "home," the preoedipal space of freedom conditioned by the
mother's bounty and body, becomes foreign: Oedipus means that it is
no longer legal to lay your head there. The lesson of the uncanny is
that

> whenever a man dreams of a place or a country and says to
> himself, while he is still dreaming: "this place is familiar to me,
> I've been here before," we may interpret the place as being his
> mother's genitals or her body. In this case too, then, the *unheimlich*
> is what was once *heimisch*, familiar; the prefix *un-* is the token of
> repression.[7]

Yet, despite the analytic knowledge that the mother's body is the
homiest place of all, the theory of the slip depends upon making the
pregnant—that is, the most specifically *motherly* body—uncanny. The
theory insists upon calling home a lost and foreign place. But the
native and the foreign are not as far apart as they seem. The connection
between them is evident in the way that the mother's body asserts
itself as a constant and necessary coordinate in reference to which
psychoanalysis is written.

4

The Body of the
Mother Tongue

Here and there, home and the foreign, the native tongue and the citation of classic texts come up again in reference to sexuality and a woman's body in chapter 3 of *The Psychopathology of Everyday Life*, "The Forgetting of Names and Sets of Words." In the first example of this chapter a slip takes place in the speaker's mother tongue, which is German, as an example of the way

> that the forgetting of poetry in one's own language could very well have motives similar to the forgetting of single elements from a set of words in a foreign tongue. (15)

This assertion opens the way to related ideas. One is that there is a paradoxical closeness between the home language and the foreign language, at least as far as regards the ways that they manifest the unconscious; both the native and the foreign tongue can help produce slips that disturb authoritative discourse. Another idea is that poetry has a specific function in the theorizing of parapraxis. The "single elements" from foreign languages that up until this chapter have served as examples for Freud are the proper name Signorelli, from the first chapter, and the indefinite pronoun *aliquis*, from the second; the latter comes from a poem (the *Aeneid*), but the former does not.

Foreign words do not have to be poetic in order to operate in slips—or perhaps poetry itself is a kind of foreign language. The introductory words in the previous extract indicate that poetry, even in one's native tongue, has a function similar to that of a foreign language. The memorization of a canonical poetic text is an attempt to make the words of another one's own. To cite such a text, as I tried to show in the discussion of Freud's use of Fliess's Goethe quotation or in Freud's friend's quotation of the *Aeneid*, is to enter into a complicated economy of identifications and authorities. The poetic text inhabits a space that is hard to localize between home and foreign.

The friend who suggested some kind of similarity between forgetting poetry in the home language and forgetting words from foreign languages also volunteered to be the subject of an experiment to determine the validity of his theory. He decided upon Goethe's poem "The Bride of Corinth" as his text. The friend liked the poem and knew some of it by heart, writes Freud. But

> at the beginning of his reproduction he was overcome by a rather remarkable uncertainty. "Does it run 'Travelling from Corinth to Athens,'" he asked, "or 'Travelling to Corinth from Athens'?" I also had a moment's hesitation, until I laughingly observed that the title of the poem "The Bride of Corinth" left no doubt which way the young man was travelling. (15)

These traveling men are, at least for a moment, not sure where they are going. Poetry has disturbed their sense of direction and confused their orientation, particularly, as in the other cases, in regard to sexuality. Because of the friend's confusion, it is hard to tell where the point of origin is. The character in the poem who is traveling from Athens to Corinth is a bridegroom who is trying to get to his bride. The poem is about a man who is on a voyage to a woman from a foreign place. The title, "The Bride of Corinth," identifies the bride, the woman, with the city of Corinth. Corinth is thus the location of femininity, and Athens, whence the man comes, is the starting point of masculinity. The friend's uncertainty, which he shares with Freud, in deciding between "from Corinth to Athens" or "to Corinth from Athens," is remarkable because it shows the friend and Freud unable to decide where they, as men, are situated in the geography of sexuality.

To recite "From Corinth to Athens" puts the friend in the place of the bride, in a way similar to that of the other friend who finds himself identifying with Dido, the wronged woman, in the *aliquis* chapter; all three men are in a situation in which they have lost the bearings that mark the boundaries of their heterosexual masculinity. This difficulty occurs immediately, with the very first verse of the poem, in the context of an experiment meant to show whether poetry in the native tongue will manifest slips in a way similar to the way foreign words do. The confusion here would seem to be a good example of the contagiousness of the phenomenon of parapraxis; the consequence of a scientific and intellectual desire to investigate slips *is* a slip that immediately grounds itself in the tenuousness of gender identifications. That the uncertainty should affect both men so completely (even if for only a moment) is particularly interesting, especially since the confusion is connected with a wedding. Marriage is a moment of legal definition that depends upon and enforces the distinction between man and woman. Nontraditional ceremonies of commitment between same-sex couples notwithstanding, marriage in the West is a legal and sometimes religious inscription of a text that determines the legitimate transfer of property and of possible descendants, based on a heterosexual relationship. Its sine qua non is the presence and spoken consent of a man and a woman whose gendered social identities and functions are probably never more clearly differentiated than they are at the marriage ceremony itself. Regardless of whatever else may be going on, the guests at a wedding can tell the difference between the bride and the groom, because that is the whole point.

The confusion of gender in this "reproduction" of the first line of the poem is the foundation for further labyrinthine errors. The friend makes a mistake in the second stanza of the poem. He says:

Aber wird er auch willkommen scheinen,
Jetzt, wo jeder Tag was Neues bringt?
Denn er ist noch Heide mit den Seinen
Und sie sind Christen und—getauft.

[But will he in fact seem welcome,
Now, when every day brings something new?
For he is still a heathen with his kindred
And they are Christians and—baptized.]

Both of them seem to know that there is something wrong with the second line of the stanza, and Freud writes:

The correct version runs:

Aber wird er auch willkommen scheinen,
Wenn er teuer nicht die Gunst erkauft?

[But will he in fact seem welcome
if he does not buy the favor dearly?]

But there is more to be corrected than Freud tells us. Strachey's notes
add that

> In addition to the introduction of the completely alien second line,
> which is discussed in the next paragraph, the third and fourth
> lines have been slightly misquoted. They should run:
>
> > Er ist noch ein Heide mit den Seinen
> > Und sie sind schon Christen und getauft.
>
> > [He is still a heathen with his kindred
> > and they are already Christians and baptized.]

(16)

The transformations are difficult to follow, but what they show is that
the whole process of quotation here is a mess. The colleague and Freud
cannot get the first verse right. Then the colleague misquotes the second stanza, and Freud corrects him only partially and incorrectly. The
problem of authority here is very hazy because of Freud's incorrect
correction. The men could not fix what they felt was wrong with the
second stanza, and so

> hurried to the bookcase to get hold of Goethe's poems, and found
> to our surprise that the second line of the stanza had a completely
> different wording, which had, as it were, been expelled from my
> colleague's memory and replaced by something that did not seem
> to belong.

If Freud and the friend had a printed version of Goethe's text, then
why didn't Freud correct the rest of the friend's errors in his essay?
(The original German text of *The Psychopathology of Everyday Life* does
not correct what Strachey calls the "slight misquotations" but, rather,
only the second line.)[1] At least one reason might be that the multiplication of errors is so unmanageable that it would render interpretation
impossible. Freud chooses to focus on a replacement of meaning,
rather than an alteration of syntax—despite the fact that it was precisely a change in syntax that merited his attention in the *aliquis* anec-

dote. Also, the profusion of errors in the quotation (one might say that the colleague murders it, the way some people are said to murder foreign languages [see my later discussion of *anekTode*]) may be seen itself as symptomatic. Neither the colleague nor Freud could fix this one—each for his own reasons.

The friend willingly analyzes his error. He connects the line he invented with the good news and fortune that he has been having in regard to his medical practice. He thinks that the prosperity to which his invention alludes is also connected to the words he repressed. "If he does not buy the favour dearly" refers to a marriage proposal that he had made once before and which, since he was now more prosperous, he was thinking of making again. But he was disturbed to think that, if he were to be accepted this time, "some sort of calculation tipped the scale both then and now." (17).

Freud writes: "This struck me as intelligible, even without my needing to know further particulars. But I continued with my questions." Why did he continue, if the answer seemed satisfactory? The next question he asked was whether there was also a problem of "differences in religious belief like those that play an important part in the poem." There was not, but the question elicits another slight misquotation from the colleague:

Sieh sie an genau!
Morgen ist sie grau.

[Look on her carefully.
Tomorrow she will be gray.]

The friend has an additional problem with his prospective wife, which is that she is "rather older" than he. Altogether, it does not sound like a recipe for happiness, especially considering the friend's misquotation, which this time Freud accurately corrects. The *sie* of the verse really refers to a lock of the *groom's* hair that he has given to the bride; she tells him that on the morrow it will be the only part of his hair that is not gray (17–18 n. 2). Again the friend's errors mark an inability to distinguish between the bride and the groom and to identify where he belongs in the economy of gender.

A similar problem of self-location surfaces for Freud, but this time more in regard to religion than to sexuality. Freud's misquotation in

The Psychopathology of Everyday Life of the last two lines of the first stanza shows, as does the friend's answer to Freud's excessive question, that the question of difference of religion was a sticking point here not for him but, rather, for Freud. Like the undercurrent in the *aliquis* example, this may be a reaction to the anti-Semitism that was so operative in Freud's time and which was understood to be one of the reasons why it took so long for the University of Vienna to name him a full professor. According to Peter Gay's biography,

> While Jews, even those who refused the profitable refuge of baptism, continued to rise to positions of eminence in the Austrian medical profession, the spreading infection of anti-Semitism did not leave influential bureaucrats untouched.[2]

Baptism was a way for a Jew to circumvent, to an extent, the bureaucratic baffles erected in Freud's Vienna. In 1897 Karl Lueger, a man who had made anti-Semitism an important part of his campaign, was elected mayor of Vienna, "seal[ing] the bankruptcy of Austrian liberalism with irrevocable finality."[3] He was still mayor when Freud began work toward *The Psychopathology of Everyday Life*. The verses

> Will he in fact seem welcome
> For he is still a heathen with his kindred
> and they are Christians and baptized,

understood in the context of fin de siècle Vienna, are a not very subtle anti-Semitic statement. The uncertainty of his welcome, and the hope that he would be let in even though unwelcome, might produce the same sensation of being neither here nor there for a Jewish professional that Freud's colleague felt while trying to locate himself in respect to marriage. Anti-Semitism literally made Freud's professional definition difficult and inhibited, for a while at least, his accession to a professorship—that is, to a position of authority.

The concerns of Freud and the younger man coalesce around the center of confusion in the anecdote, that of the location of the bride. Despite the fact that she is a protagonist of Goethe's poem, she is only ancillary to a larger story, which is that of Freud and his "younger colleague" and their theorizing of parapraxis. "The Bride of Corinth" is a text through which the men engage each other, the younger colleague offering to adopt a subordinate position, as experimental object of analysis, to help further the older, authoritative man's research. His confusion makes him a bride—not of that other scientist, Frankenstein, but of Freud. The situation is not unlike the relationship between Freud, as junior colleague, and Fliess, as authority, and the way that that relationship makes possible Freud's misquotation of *Faust*. In the errant quotation of a poetic text or of a foreign language, a younger man puts himself in the position of the feminine in reference to an older or more authoritative man. This hom(m)osexuality constructs itself to exclude women but still uses the idea of woman or women's bodies as a space through which it may narrate itself. The use of the foreign and the poetic, by way of their implicit identification with the feminine, helps to maintain the continuity of a hierarchy based on the power of dominant (older) man over subordinate (younger) man. But in these three cases (*Faust*, *aliquis*, and "The Bride of Corinth") the attempt to ensure the integrity of the male homosocial bond by means of submission to textual authority—that is, by putting the foreign or poetic words of another in one's own mouth—subverts itself in the slip.

In all three cases younger men, who ultimately seek the position of authority of the older man to whom they (for the moment) submit, attempt to leave the mother tongue behind; the structure that they want to inherit is based on the fiction of male primacy, and the mother tongue is too constant a reminder of the woman at their origin to be used in these ceremonial utterances. The use of the foreign and canonical poetic words starts out as a way of repressing or avoiding association with whatever is feminine (i.e., not dominant or not convincing) in the mother tongue; to cite *uncritically*, for political or academic purposes, the canonical texts of Western culture is to attempt, by using their words, to identify with the men who wrote them and canonized them. The quotations that I have examined so far have in common that uncritical use; they are never subjected to a process of analysis. Instead, they are reified and taken literally as texts that are meant unequivocally to reinforce the arguments in which they appear; to cite Virgil or Goethe is, etymologically and by definition, to speak with authority.

The effect of this uncritical use of citation is always to place authority in the other: one's own words are never (in this system) as authoritative as those that belong to someone else. A paradoxical relationship arises with respect to the words of the other. On the one hand, their use can be a way of identifying with authority, but, on the other hand, to use the words of another instead of one's own is to place oneself in a submissive (and thus not authoritative) position. Additionally, it must be remembered that not all foreign words are authoritative, and these latter more immediately produce the submissive position. What I would like to focus on here is the way that the use of the words of another—foreign words, culturally fixed texts, academic citations—disturbs categories of authority and the notion of dominance itself.

Two texts that are in varying degrees marginal to *The Psychopathology of Everyday Life* may help to articulate these disturbances. One of these texts is the first anecdote related in the essay on "Fetishism," "the most extraordinary case" that Freud had seen, in which

> a young man had exalted a certain sort of "shine on the nose" into a fetishistic precondition. The surprising explanation of this was that the patient had been brought up in a English nursery but had later come to Germany, where he forgot his mother-tongue almost completely. The fetish, which originated from his earliest childhood, had to be understood in English, not German. The "shine on the nose" ["Glanz auf der Nase"]—was in reality a *"glance* at the nose." The nose was thus the fetish, which, incidentally, he endowed at will with the luminous shine which was not perceptible to others.[4]

A "fetishistic precondition" means that the man could only obtain sexual gratification for himself if the *Glanz* was present. His physiological sexual response depends upon the *Glanz*. What is so astonishing about this fetish is that it exists in and because of language, that it exists precisely in the tension between the mother tongue and (what was, at least at the beginning) a foreign language, and that the word itself makes possible a bodily response. Instead of what happens in hysteria, in which the body takes over the symbolic process of language, here what happens is that language is made to function like a body. The word *Glanz*, which means "shine" in German, is a homophone for the English word *glance*. In the *"Glanz auf der Nase"* example two languages are spoken at once. Together they make possible a connection with the mother's body by means of the survival of her almost—but not quite—forgotten language in the language of adulthood. I am not sure whether this body is the imaginary body of the phallic mother or one that might precede that formulation. If, as Freud writes, "The nose was thus the fetish," then the *Glanz* may help to determine it but is not the fetish itself. *Glanz*, articulated in the foreign language and reminiscent of the mother tongue, represses, but also remembers, the mother's body.

A close reading of the transference of meaning occurring in this use of *Glanz* suggests a comparison with Roland Barthes's analysis of Balzac's short story "Sarrasine." Sarrasine is a sculptor who has fallen in love with the castrato singer La Zambinella, not realizing that she is a he . . . more or less. Barthes says that, according to "customary French onomastics," the protagonist's name would be spelled Sarrazine and that its mutation indicates something. In fact, this misplaced z is

> the letter of mutilation: . . . the letter of deviation, . . . the first letter of La Zambinella, the initial of castration, so that by this orthographical error committed in the middle of his name, in the center of his body, Sarrasine receives the Zambinellan Z in its true sense—the wound of deficiency.[5]

Z, for Sarrasine, is the mark of his own castration anxiety: the threat that has not yet been carried out but whose whisper is always just barely audible. S is its reverse, which is the illusion of masculine wholeness and integrity that the phallus represents but which, paradoxically, depends for its very existence upon the castration that it reflects.

Something even more deviant is going on in the relationship between *Glanz* and *glance*. In *Glanz*, the z that in its absence from Sarrasine is "the wound of deficiency" is *present*. This z is the acknowledgment of the woman's castration that lurks just beneath the surface of fetishism: the fetish covers up, but does not entirely obliterate, the repressed knowledge that the mother has no penis.[6] This belief in her castration is the moment of separation from the mother, and in Freudian theory is related to the Oedipus complex, during which the boy child learns to defer his love for his mother and to redirect it toward other women. The z in *Glanz* is not, obviously, the same thing as the c in *glance*. C curves another way; unlike the s in *Sarrasine*, it cannot and does not attempt to reflect z. It is a letter whose meaning depends upon the space it makes that is neither inside nor outside it. It is not a hole and not a zero. It has definition and boundaries, but it does not cut anything out. It is one of the easiest letters to write. Needless to say, it is a part of castration—but castration is not a part of it. This *c* might be an alphabetical symbol for the female body that precedes and exceeds the definitions of its castration.

Freud's fetishist took the *c* of *glance* and turned it into the *z* of *Glanz*. His phrase takes a way of seeing (*c*-ing, after all) or of moving quickly across something (two definitions of the word in English) and turns it into an insubstantial light effect (a shine) to be looked *at* or through. In this respect his translation of *glance* into *Glanz* may be seen as a way of distancing himself from his mother's body, which he found too terrifyingly different from his own. Making one language stand in for another can be fetishistic. In this case, in order to fit in with established systems, the man literally turns his mother tongue into a foreign tongue. Like the little Freud in the screen memory about the yellow flowers, the fetishist had no choice in the matter of leaving the English nursery that was his first home. But his mother tongue is only "almost" forgotten. Within the elaborate and thorough system of castration and development, a trace of contact with a mother tongue that does *not* encode the law of the father, but nevertheless makes sense, still articulates itself. In this case, through the use of the second language Freud's patient not only distances himself from his mother but also finds a way back to her.

Glanz, between the mother and the foreign tongue, functions as a metaphor—both for castration and for the body of the mother that precedes it. Lacan states that "the symptom *is* a metaphor"[7] and that the formula for metaphor, as well as for poetry, is "*one word for another.*"[8] One word for another is also part of the process of translation, whether of unconscious to conscious or from mother to foreign tongue. In reference to these activities, Barbara Johnson writes that "through the foreign language we renew our love-hate relationship with our mother tongue," facing and railing against all of its inadequacies, publicly playing out "the scene of linguistic castration," ultimately wishing that "we could have stayed at home" but nevertheless acknowledging "the impossibility of staying at home with the mother tongue."[9] To stay home, to remain in the womb, is to suffocate and to defeat the will of the mother, which is to make us live. But to need to move away from home is not the same thing as to assert, "You can't go home again." To eradicate connection with the mother, to leave her entirely behind, is as impossible and lethal as staying home for good. It is possible, if confusing, to go back and forth. For us, as for Freud's fetishist, the foreign language is a method for leaving mother behind. It is also, inevitably and often unexpectedly, a way back home. In the *Glanz* example, metaphor in its poetic function, castration, and the unconscious all lead back to the mother's body.

The fetishist's take on *Glanz* and *glance* is a very useful example of the function of the slip in meaning—not one thing instead of another but, rather, things multiply, fully, and simultaneously. It is also, thus, an example of why the slip can seem so threatening. Like the other examples in *The Interpretation of Dreams, Jokes and Their Relation to the Unconscious,* and *The Psychopathology of Everyday Life,* the *Glanz* is part of

> a web of examples whose development is inscribed in the formulas of connexion and substitution . . . these are the formulas we give to the signifier in its *transference* function.[10]

As Lacan pointed out in 1966, such a use of words is "what provoked resistance to psychoanalysis from the outset" because, by altering "the relation between man and the signifier," it "modif[ies] the moorings that anchor his being."[11]

But there is more to it. The unavoidable multiple meanings of the slip do not only "modify the moorings" of the ship of the Man, which is patriarchy; they demonstrate that the metaphor of moorings and a ship without them adrift on a chaotic miasma (Lacan's *man,* civilization, the state, tossed about on annihilating feminine liquids) is one of the more tired and inaccurate ones in the Book. To speak more than one language, and to slip, does not destroy the symbolic but, rather, complicates and enriches it and proves that there is more than one way to make sense. It is not only because the unconscious operates in the slip, but also because psychoanalytic and popular discourses are constrained by their still evident adherence to binary oppositions to figure the slip as feminine, that alterations in the relationship between *man* and the signifier, such as those evidenced by slips, have the potential to interrupt and rechannel history. The slip in and between mother and foreign tongues unhinges dominance because it articulates an otherwise repressed symbolic function that has power but is not "masculine," in that it does not participate in erasing other discourses but, rather, makes itself known with and through them. It is inscribed as feminine because it is disruptive of univocal discourse. But its power and implications exceed the feminine role it has been written into.

A further example of how this feminine role is written for the slip and then how that femininity disrupts the masculine discourse that invented it is in the second of the two marginal examples that I would like to discuss. This one appears in one of Freud's footnotes to chapter 8 of *The Psychopathology of Everyday Life*, "Bungled Actions," and refers to the ways that unconscious suicides come about. Freud writes:

> Even a *conscious* intention of committing suicide chooses its time, means, and opportunity; and it is quite in keeping with this that an *unconscious* intention should wait for a precipitating occasion which can take over a part of the causation and, by engaging the subject's defensive forces, can liberate the intention from their pressure. (181)

In other words, an unconscious desire to commit suicide, which would normally be squelched by conscious prohibitions of the act, waits for an opportunity—a horseback ride, a car trip—in which an "accident" might allow it to be fulfilled. As a further explanation, Freud supplies a footnote that appears at the end of the passage previously cited. What is curious about the footnote is that it draws parallels between suicide and rape:

> After all, the case is no different from that of a sexual assault upon a woman, where the man's attack cannot be repelled by her full muscular strength because a portion of her unconscious impulses meets the attack with encouragement. It is said, as we know, that a situation of this kind paralyses a woman's strength; all we need to do is to add the reasons for this paralysis. (181 n. 1)

The example in the text of *The Psychopathology of Everyday Life* is of an officer who rode in a race, fell from his horse, and died of the injuries that he sustained. His behavior previous to the accident had shown him to be depressed and world-weary; he had even had fits of sobbing in front of his fellow military men. He had recently decided to enlist in active fighting; he had previously enjoyed riding but now held himself back from it. Before the race that killed him, in which he was socially compelled to participate, "he expressed gloomy forbodings" (181–82). The idea is that a part of him, however small and repressed, wanted to commit suicide and that the race provided a situation in which the unconscious wish might weaken the conscious effort to stay alive.

In the case of rape the situation is not precisely analogous. A suicide is a person who kills him or herself; suicide breaks down the subject-object distinction, and the one who acts is the recipient of the action. Rape may be referred to in English as "a fate worse than death," but, in fact, relinquishing physical resistance to rape is one way, often, of surviving it. Rapists are sometimes satisfied with less than killing their victim. A suicidal wish is not. Further, suicides may wish to harm other people by their actions, but, by definition, they only kill themselves. This is not what happens in a rape. In a rape there are two or more people, and the conscious will of the aggressor contradicts the conscious will of the victim. The rapist only wants to rape women who don't want him to rape them. He is the subject, the victim is the object, and the rape itself is a scenario originated by the rapist, not by the victim. A woman does not rape herself; men rape women. Because of the specific difference in agency and subject-object relations in the cases of suicide and rape, it is significant that Freud should write that they are "no different."[12] Here again gender makes the difference. It is in the moment of rape when masculinity most graphically asserts its dominance over femininity (instances of men raping other men in rituals of dominance and hazing confirm this). The mechanics of rape are that the female, or feminized body, must be penetrated—not necessarily by a part of the rapist's body but by something. Rape and suicide thus do have in common, for their victims, a loss of control over the boundaries between inside and outside and a destructive transgression of their subjectivity. But it is necessarily in rape, not in suicide, that the question of gender, of the enacting of the dominance of masculine over feminine, is crucial.

Nevertheless, Freud builds his theory of the operation of the unconscious in "accidental" suicides on the analogy of the operation of the unconscious in weakening a woman's resistance to rape. There is no clear parallelism between the terms of the analogy. What Freud's phrase "no different" leads to is an equation between a man who cannot keep from acting upon himself and a woman who cannot keep from being acted upon. Because of the structure of Freud's text, in which the rape analogy appears in a footnote, we can read that analogy as an explanation of what happens in suicide, but we cannot read what happens in suicide as an explanation of what happens in rape. If the suicide dies because the unconscious weakens the conscious and if the woman is raped because the unconscious weakens the conscious, then the inevitable result of using the footnote as an explanation of the main text is that the soldier is somehow "raped" by the unconscious and, thus, feminized in relation to it. The more usual structure—conscious = rational = masculine, unconscious = irrational = feminine—is here reoriented, with the unconscious assuming a masculine relationship to a feminized conscious. Freud's analogy takes structures of gender and subjectivity for a hair-raising ride.

In the second lecture on parapraxes in the *New Introductory Lectures on Psychoanalysis* Freud likens the analytic scene to a courtroom, with the therapist the judge and the patient the accused:

> When someone charged with an offence confesses his deed to the judge, the judge believes his confession; but if he denies it, the judge does not believe him. If it were otherwise, there would be no administration of justice, and in spite of occasional errors we must allow that the system works.[13]

The footnote about rape and the unconscious continues with a courtroom example drawn from *Don Quixote*, which was, according to Jones, one of Freud's favorite books. He had read it

> first in boyhood. Now [ca. 1885] his friend Herzig gave him a luxurious copy, one he had longed to own, which contained the Doré illustrations. He had always been extraordinarily fond of the stories, and on re-reading them found them the most entertaining and enjoyable of anything he knew.[14]

In the story that Freud selects, Sancho Panza is the analyst, and a woman who has come before him with a complaint about having been raped is the patient. Freud's version of her case history is as follows:

A woman dragged a man before the judge alleging he had robbed her of her honour by violence. In compensation Sancho gave her a full purse of money which he took from the accused; but after the woman's departure he gave him permission to pursue her and snatch his purse back again from her. The two returned struggling, the woman priding herself on the fact that the villain had not been able to take the purse from her. Thereupon Sancho declared: "If you had defended your honour with half the determination with which you have defended this purse, the man could not have robbed you of it."

Since Freud has explained that rape paralyzes a woman's resistance because "a portion of her unconscious impulses meets the act with encouragement," he says that "the ingenious judgement delivered by Sancho Panza as governor of his island is psychologically unjust"; that is, Sancho is a bad analyst. The logic is that the woman can defend her money better than she can her honor because there is no pleasure to be had from the act of losing money but always at least some association of pleasure with the experience of genital contact. That wish for pleasure would then inhibit resistance to rape. Sancho is a bad analyst because he does not take this into account.

Despite the fact that they are both exchange objects in similar economies, a woman's body and money are not the same. Sancho does not see this, but Freud does, if only in reference to the woman's ability to defend each entity from encroachment. But neither Freud nor Sancho sees the difference between a woman's body and money in reference to the rapist; both analysts note that the *woman* did not protect her body as well as she did her money. But I would like to turn the question around and to suggest that perhaps the *man* could not get the purse away from the *woman* because *he* did not want the money as much as he wanted to rape her. A rapist's conscious and unconscious intentions are much more of a determinant in whether a woman will be raped than are *her* unconscious wishes. Furthermore, in the text of *Don Quixote* it is clear that the woman has come to court precisely in order to get some kind of financial restitution. When he is asked for his version of what happened, the man says to Sancho:

el diablo, que todo lo añasca y todo lo cuece, hizo que yogásemos juntos; paguéle lo soficiente, y ella, mal contenta, asió de mí, y no me ha dejado hasta traerme a este puesto.

[the Devil, the author of all mischief, made us couple together. I paid her sufficient, but she wasn't content and caught hold of me and wouldn't let me go until she had dragged me to this place.][15]

She does not contradict his narrative. She is happy with the purse full of money that she gets because it is a substitute for the real economic value (in marriage) of her virginity. She can defend it from him because he does not want it enough to fight her for it. There is no enforcement of gender privilege in taking her money; there is in taking her body against her will. The man is responsible for the rape, as the suicide (as both conscious and unconscious entity) is for his own death.

It is difficult to determine why Freud chose to use this anecdote. There is another one, equally if not more well known, that makes the same point. A woman engages Napoleon at a party and complains to him that one of his officers has raped her. Napoleon gives her his sword and tells her to try to put it back in its scabbard, which he keeps waving back and forth. Of course, the woman fails, and she is told that, if she had kept moving like the scabbard did, no officer could have had his way with her. One assumes that she stalks off, furious. This anecdote lacks the comparison with money that the one from Cervantes makes available; it also lacks the appeal that literary texts held for Freud. But many other great works of literature deal with rape in a similar way. *Don Quixote* has a particular attraction, which is that it is, at least conventionally, a narrative about a madman and the definition of madness; that is, it is a kind of case history. Also, Freud had in his youth a strong attachment to and identification with the characters of other of Cervantes's works. In particular, as schoolboys, he and his inseparable friend Eduard Silberstein taught themselves Spanish and used it as a secret language. Freud called himself Cipión after one of the two main animal characters in Cervantes's exemplary novel *The Colloquy of the Dogs*; Silberstein was Berganza, the other dog.[16]

Cipión is analytical and criticizes Berganza's narration of his life during the story; that is, Cipión, who speaks little and listens much, is in the position of an analyst and Berganza of a patient.[17] The two characters are considered by Hispanists to be parallels of Don Quixote and Sancho and, especially, of the development of their intensely dialogic relationship in the second part of *Don Quixote*. If Sancho, according to Freud, is an unjust psychological judge and Freud is correcting him, then Freud is again in the position of Don Quixote, who corrects Sancho's linguistic errors throughout the novel. Similarly, if Sancho is an inaccurate analyst and Freud is pointing out his error, then Freud is again identified with Don Quixote. At any rate, his remarks in letters to Fliess around the time of the writing of *The Psychopathology of Everyday Life* make it clear that he felt that his psychoanalytic work was somewhat quixotic: Freud, like Don Quixote, was somewhat out of synch with his times—but by being ahead of them, rather than behind.

It should also be remembered that the only unremitting delusion of Don Quixote, one that persists until the end of the book, is his fantasy of Dulcinea. His mission as a knight-errant would be meaningless if it were not for the image of femininity that he invents. True to the tradition of courtly love, his whole chivalric process depends upon his theorizing about, but never arriving at, Dulcinea. He must not know her, because to know her would bring his whole epistemological edifice—which is founded not on an understanding of the experiences of real women but, rather, on a male fantasy of of what femininity should be—crashing down. *The Colloquy of the Dogs* is a conversation between two male canines; *Don Quixote* is a conversation between two men, in which Dulcinea's function is to make possible the traveling dialogues of Don Quixote and Sancho. If I may borrow the technique of drawing analogies with *Don Quixote* from Freud, I would suggest that the way that Freudian theory veers away from femininity and the preoedipal and focuses instead always on the "boy child," is in part determined by this quixotic structure, in which woman is a utility that makes it possible for men to talk to one another about themselves. That is why what the woman in the rape anecdote wants is not taken into account. The famous Freudian question "Was will das Weib?" (What does woman want?) is a question that men address to one another but not to women.[18] The woman in the footnote is only there to facilitate the making of the story about the cavalry officer—who is a *caballero*, a horseman, like Don Quixote.

Nevertheless, she exceeds her role and derails theory. The analogy between suicide and rape does not work, or, rather, it causes the theory to slip, because a woman's responsibility in a case of rape is different from a man's responsibility for his suicide. What happens in practice to women's bodies exceeds the limits of a theory of the unconscious based on a fictionalized idea of femininity.

Living through the Slip

The chapter on the forgetting of sets of words in which "The Bride of Corinth" and the *Don Quixote* examples appear marks the beginning of a change of structure for *The Psychopathology of Everyday Life*. The first two chapters each present only one example of a slip, and neither chapter changes much from edition to edition. But the same is not true of the third chapter. From the first edition to the eleventh, it undergoes many additions of anecdotes. Also, it is the first chapter to include anecdotes that Freud collected from friends and colleagues, instead of just using examples from his own experience. For the critic of *The Psychopathology of Everyday Life* this endless multiplication of anecdotes produces a situation like the one that Freud faces before the many errors in his young friend's version of "The Bride of Corinth." The sheer number of slips makes any kind of comprehensive interpretation impossible. The book went through eleven German editions in Freud's lifetime; seven of the editions are "enlarged." It was first published in two numbers of the *Monatsschrift für Psychiatrie und Neurologie* in 1901. In its first appearance in book form in 1904 *The Psychopathology of Everyday Life* is ninety-two pages long; its final versions all have more than three hundred pages. It is true that *The Interpretation of Dreams* and the *Three Essays on the Theory of Sexuality* also show many additions, but these are

> important enlargements or corrections of clinical findings and theoretical conclusions. In *The Psychopathology of Everyday Life* almost the whole of the basic explanations and theories were already present in the earliest editions; the great mass of what was added later consisted merely in extra examples and illustrations (partly produced by Freud himself but largely by his friends and pupils) to throw further light upon what he had already discussed. (x)

What started out as a theory about the functioning of "primary and secondary" thought processes, buttressed by a few carefully selected examples from Freud's own experience, in which those examples are smoothly woven into the main text, ends up as an excessive pastiche of anecdotes. One wonders why Freud wanted to add so many stories to the collection. In the editor's introduction to *The Psychopathology of Everyday Life* James Strachey suggests that "no doubt he felt particular pleasure both in the anecdotes themselves and in being presented with such widespread confirmation of his views" (x). Freud does call the "task of collecting and analysing slips of the tongue" "amusing" (67). Later in the introduction Strachey refers to "the special affection with which Freud regarded parapraxes," giving them sometimes "a preference even over dreams" (xiii). Strachey attributes their "peculiar attraction" for Freud to the idea that they would be useful in proving his theory of complete psychic determinism in which "it should be possible in theory to discover the psychical determinants of every smallest detail of the processes of the mind" (xiv). But the phrases "particular pleasure," "special affection," and "peculiar attraction" mark the slips (at least in Strachey's mind) as producing some kind of perverse delight for Freud. The student and translator is not disturbed because his authority makes slips but, rather, that, in the writing of his book on slips, he slips up; the excessiveness of the later editions of *The Psychopathology of Everyday Life* has a disappointing effect on the reader, who has come to expect a perfection of style from Freud. This "reader cannot help feeling sometimes that the wealth of new examples interrupts and even confuses the main stream of the underlying argument" (x). Freud is taking some kind of pleasure from mounting up the tally of anecdotes, and the reader cannot share it—at least not if that reader is looking for a conventional kind of clarity, or a strictly linear argument.

Freud's pleasure in the excesses of *The Psychopathology of Everyday Life* is at times marked by some ambivalence, too. At the beginning of chapter 6, "Misreadings and Slips of the Pen," he says, "I shall confine myself here to reporting a few carefully analysed examples, and shall make no attempt to cover every aspect of the phenomena" (106). In the first edition of the book he stays true to this promise, providing only three examples each of misreadings and slips of the pen; all of these, like all of the other examples from the 1901 and 1904 texts, are Freud's own slips. But by the tenth (1924) edition, despite the fact that the promise of brevity still begins the chapter, the number of stories of misreadings has multiplied to thirteen and the number of slips of the pen to twenty-three.

The same process of expansion may be observed in other chapters of the book, with the exception of the Signorelli, the *aliquis,* and the screen memory chapters (chapters 1, 2, and 4). There is a change from the conservative, expository use of the anecdote in those three chapters and the excessive, nonlinear cataloging of examples in the rest of the book. The fact that Freud says that he will "confine [himself] to . . . a few carefully analysed examples"[1] indicates that he is aware of the potential of the book to spin out of control; he is aware of the excess but cannot seem to stop it. Later, in "Errors" (chapter 10), Freud writes:

> To avoid confining myself entirely to my own errors, I shall report a few examples that might indeed have been included just as well among slips of the tongue and bungled actions; this is, however, a matter of indifference, since all these forms of parapraxis are equivalent to one another. (222)

In the 1907 edition these examples really were few: there were only three, the classical minimum (and maximum) for a convincing argument. But Freud could not stick to the limit, and this part of the chapter, by 1920, has seventeen examples, which are by no means few. The multiplication of examples has several effects. It disrupts the order of the book and shows its randomness; a slip that appears in the errors chapter could as easily have been in two other ones, so what does the chapter division mean? A little later, in reference to some examples of confusion between names, Freud says, "They might of course have been equally well included in other chapters of the book" (224). The anecdotes do not obey the conventions of expository organization; they slide between categories and chapter boundaries. Also, the supposed randomness of their location in the text is undercut by Freud's assertions, in the last chapter on determinism, that all thoughts have a traceable meaning. There is a reason why Freud decided to put a certain anecdote in the errors chapter and not in the chapter on bungled actions, and to the analytical reader it is not "a matter of indifference." The order supplied by Freud, he admits in the chapter on determinism, signifies. But he will not tell us what it means.

The large number of examples has another effect as well; it helps to camouflage and protect Freud. If he were to confine himself to his own errors, then the charge might be leveled against him that it was only his peculiar psyche that produced these effects and that they do not exist in other people; this would contradict the whole purpose of *The Psychopathology of Everyday Life,* which is to show that the unconscious is at work in everyone. The first benefit of introducing many anecdotes concerned with and contributed by other people is thus to provide a chorus of agreement with Freud. It is also an example of some of the effects of the pedagogy of parapraxis, which I discuss in my first chapter. By exposing his own slips, Freud elicits similar stories of failure of mastery from others. If he can err and learn from it, so can his students. But this process is not exclusively benevolent, particularly when confession is used tactically, not as a way of subverting mastery but, rather, as a paradoxical way of achieving it.

In *The Psychopathology of Everyday Life* Freud may tell about his own slips, but then he also tells about the slips of others. And when his colleagues and friends contribute slips, they not only confess their own but also tattle on their patients. The balance of power in this economy of mastery and submission is rarely in the patients' favor, because they are not able to choose whether they will become characters in an anecdote or how they will appear if they do. The rule "Tell on yourself if you want to tell on others" is rigorously applied; every practicing psychoanalyst who contributes to *The Psychopathology of Everyday Life* narrates at least one of his own slips before he is permitted to include one about a patient. If, in this regard, it may by said that the analyst's confession of a slip functions in *The Psychopathology of Everyday Life* as a trace of the training analysis, which is (among other things) a required period of submission to authority necessary to accede to that same authority, then it is possible that the anecdotes about patients' slips work as minute but dense case histories. They narrate how the symptom occurs and what its context is, analyze it, and terminate the case, generally with an elegant fillip. Analyses of slips are especially satisfying because it seems possible to complete them. Their scene and content are limited, and it seems possible to leave nothing of them unanalyzed. They suggest that some question has been answered completely and with finality.

The paradoxical effect of the repetition of this scene of analytical completeness that the many anecdotes represent is, however, to fragment the book and to make a unified analysis of *it* almost impossible. Freud was aware of this; near the end he says, in regard to parapraxes and determinism, that "the indulgent reader may accordingly see in these discussions signs of the broken edges where this subject has been somewhat artificially detached from a wider context" (277). In this case what is true for the last chapter is true for most of the book; much of *The Psychopathology of Everyday Life* does indeed seem to be a composite of "broken edges."[2] Freud was conscious of its fragmentation and even seemed to anticipate with enjoyment the irritating effect it would have on its readers. In his 8 May 1901 letter to Fliess he writes: "I dislike it tremendously and hope others will do so even more. The essay is entirely without structure and contains all sorts of forbidden +++ things."[3] If the first version of *The Psychopathology of Everyday Life* is "without structure," then the whirl of additions and editions that succeed it is labyrinthine, and almost impossible to follow. Like that of a labyrinth, their complexity is notable because it is a way of hiding something, of eradicating attempts to discover that which is hidden, and, eventually, of trapping whomever enters the structure in an attempt to uncover its secrets.

In the case of *The Psychopathology of Everyday Life* it is possible that the individual broken pieces are less significant than the characteristic of fragmentation, of being "hard to follow," that dominates the reader's experience of the book. The form of *The Psychopathology of Everyday Life* is determined by two structures, the fragment and the anecdote. Multiplication and excess seem at first to be a way of proving Freud's points about the existence and operation of the unconscious. But they have another function, too. The etymology of the word *anecdote* is "that which is not given out".[4] Despite its verbal excess, *The Psychopathology of Everyday Life,* by reiterating its anecdotes, by giving too much of "that which is not given out," is holding something back. That something is connected to its fragmentary character, too.

At the same time that he was writing *The Psychopathology of Everyday Life* Freud was at work on a manuscript that he called "Dreams and Hysteria," which finally would be published under the title "Fragment of a Case of Hysteria" and is better known as "the Dora case." The most prominent point of contact between the two works is an anecdote about the name Dora in *The Psychopathology of Everyday Life,* which I will discuss later in this chapter. Many of the critics who have written on the Dora case have mentioned this anecdote, mostly look-ing for the significance of the name to Freud and how that significance might illuminate Freud's understanding of Dora and his own psychic circumstances and investments in her case.[5] In this regard *The Psycho-pathology of Everyday Life* is used as a text that might explain Dora. What I would like to do here is to show how "Fragment of an Analysis of a Case of Hysteria" impacts upon the writing of *The Psychopathology of Everyday Life*, how the excess of the latter attempts to make up for the lack that dominates the former, and to demonstrate that *The Psy-chopathology of Everyday Life* says too much because the "Fragment" cannot say enough. The tension between two Greek words, *Dora*, a "gift," and *anecdote*, "that which is not given out," may help to explain not only that psychoanalytic theory depends upon a rhetoric of misog-yny but also that it shows how misogyny may be taken apart.

The woman who would be written up as Dora first came to see Freud in the autumn of 1900. She stayed for about three months, until 31 December. At the same time that he was treating Dora, Freud was writing *The Psychopathology of Everyday Life*. After Dora's abrupt depar-ture from therapy, which Freud found both frustrating and infuriating, he began to write her case history and finished it on 24 January 1901. *The Psychopathology of Everyday Life* was not completed until sometime around 15 February. Nevertheless, the latter book was published in July and August of 1901, and "Fragment of an Analysis of a Case of Hysteria" did not appear until 1905, or four years after it was fin-ished.[6] On 25 January 1901 Freud wrote to Fliess that "Fragment" "is really a continuation of the dream book."[7] This may be true, but the fact that it was written "simultaneously"[8] with *The Psychopathology of Everyday Life* argues for a strong intertextual relationship between Dora and the slip as well. Freud was writing *The Psychopathology of Everyday Life* before, during, and after the time that he was writing the "Fragment." The mass of *The Psychopathology of Everyday Life* is like a wad of cotton that surrounds the "Fragment," both protecting and silencing it. Where *The Psychopathology of Everyday Life* is excessive and comprehensive, the "Fragment of an Analysis of a Case of Hysteria" is meager and unfinished. If the chorus of voices of agreement that Freud added to *The Psychopathology of Everyday Life* over the years is an emblem of his professional success, then the inability to say enough to complete Dora's analysis gives the impression, as many writers have noted, of failure. It cannot have been easy to publish the account of that failure; it is hard to admit that things have gone wrong. But it was a moral and ethical victory for Freud to be able to publish "Fragment of an Analysis of a Case of Hysteria," even if it was four years late, because that text shows not only that Freud was not omniscient but also that he knew he was not. Like the initial examples of his own slips in *The Psychopathology of Everyday Life*, it shows the limits of his mastery over his own consciousness and radically demythologizes him. By publishing the Dora case, Freud made it possible for others to learn from his mistakes, if they chose to.

And he still had *The Psychopathology of Everyday Life* for consolation. In the first mention of what will become Freudian slips, Freud says to Fliess that the analysis of his forgetting the name of the poet Julius Mosen is "complete, with no gaps left; unfortunately, I cannot expose it to the public anymore than my big dream."[9] Freud made up for having to conceal this anecdote with a vengeance; the many "public" anecdotes in *The Psychopathology of Everyday Life* fill the void left by discretion and resistance with many comforting noises. Another etymology of *anecdote* is "unpublished."[10] The anecdotes become a substitute for that which Freud does not publish or give out. But there is a contradiction built into the word *anecdote*. If it is by definition unpublished, then it becomes a kind of antitext, or a form of writing that erases writing. The telling of anecdotes in *The Psychopathology of Everyday Life* is a way of untelling the Dora story, which is the story of Freud's mastery slipping away. Or at least it is a way of compensating for having had to tell it. The obsessive and complete analysis of one slip after another compensates for the sense of loss and failure created by cases that elude the analyst's grasp. I am tempted to suggest that the writing of "Fragment of an Analysis of a Case of Hysteria," encased as it is, chronologically, in the writing of *The Psychopathology of Everyday Life*, makes it a part of the latter text. "Fragment" was for four years literally *an-ekdota*, unpublished, an anecdote, and anecdote is the genre par excellence of *The Psychopathology of Everyday Life*. In "Fragment" Freud states that:

> It is a rule of psycho-analytic technique that an internal connection which is still undisclosed will announce its presence by means of a contiguity—a temporal proximity—of associations; just as in writing, if "a" and "b" are put side by side, it means that the syllable "ab" is to be formed out of them.[11]

Because "Fragment" and *The Psychopathology of Everyday Life* were *written together*, in "temporal proximity," like the letters *a* and *b*, they may be read together as making a kind of composite sense. Each work has an individual meaning, but each also completes the meaning of the other in a necessarily symbiotic relationship. "Fragment" is pure anecdote, the unpublished unconscious of *The Psychopathology of Everyday Life*. And *The Psychopathology of Everyday Life*, in its hysterical excess, is a constant reminder of the "Fragment" that it was written around and over.

The title "Fragment of an Analysis of a Case of Hysteria" is somewhat deceptive; readers over the years have noticed this and refer to it insistently as the Dora case, or even just "Dora." This popular title derives from the fact that "Fragment" is, other essays notwithstanding, the Freudian text most directly concerned with the ways that a female body—as distinguished, but not necessarily separate, from femininity—can interrupt the work of theory. The "Fragment" becomes popularly known as Dora because of the agency of the woman that Freud treated: her decisions and actions, rather than Freud's, determine the outcome of the narration. Some kind of female agency that is autonomous from it redirects the text and insists on itself over and above Freud's written title.

Nevertheless, whether known as Dora or as Ida Bauer (her real name), the female subject of Freud's inquiry in the "Fragment" continues to be rewritten. I am not suggesting that the real woman that Freud treated ever gets to speak for herself either in his text or in the scholarship about it. What I will say is that, because of her decision to take herself away from Freud, the text about her has become canonized as an object lesson against mastery and that it has become so under a feminine name. The Dora case becomes for Freud and his readers an example of a kind of femininity that exceeds the definitions written for it. No amount of writing about the Dora case can tell us more than we already know, which is that Freud did not know enough, and he did not know enough because Dora took herself away. The Dora case is about a concrete female body, as opposed to an abstract notion of femininity, that eludes Freud's theorizing. It might be said that Dora is evidence of the existence of the woman, or the female body, which escapes or leaves behind the theoretical monologue. Despite the word's Greek etymology, Dora is not a gift but, rather, is a gift's opposite; she is that which is taken away. Freud's way of dealing with the Dora who will not give herself to him is to textualize her, to turn her into a "Fragment." It must be noted here that Dora is only Dora, and a fragment, to Freud and his readers; that is, she is only broken, partial, mutilated, and incomplete *as a text*. In reference to the real woman who served as that text's catalyst, *fragment* is an irrelevant term. Yet it is only by inscribing her under the title "Fragment" that she may be included in the theory of psychoanalysis.

The question of defining a fragment now arises. Is a fragment something that has lost a piece of itself, like, for example, a document whose last few pages are gone? Or is a fragment the missing piece itself, something from which the rest of the story may be inferred? The dictionary says that it is "an extant part of an unfinished or lost text" and that it comes from the Latin *frangere*, "to break."[12] If we transpose this definition into the terms of castration, that primordial tale of fragmentation, then the woman may be perceived as mutilated because she has lost the penis. But this, paradoxically, would make the penis itself a fragment—that is, something incomplete because broken off from something else. Because the penis, in terms of castration theory, is the symbol of unity and wholeness, some other fragment must be found. Since a fragment may be defined by its broken edges, by its incompleteness, the *woman's body* becomes the fragment; it is something that has broken off, or diverged from, the penis, and thus the male organ may retain its place as primary signifier. But Dora, while still a female body, does something different from what the (by definition) castrated woman is supposed to do. Instead of accustoming herself to the position of a fragment, she cuts Freud off. By removing her body from the scene of analysis, she frustrates both the questions and the answers put to her. Not only is the "Fragment of an Analysis of a Case of Hysteria" an anecdote because it is unpublished for four years, but Dora herself becomes "that which is not given out," a kind of femininity that moves beyond the broken edges of psychoanalytic theory.

The reason that Dora exceeds theory is that she insists upon her *body* as the primary etymology of her meaning. Her body means more than the theories of hysteria that Freud uses to make sense of it for himself. The meaning of her body that exceeds his interpretations of her hysteria is what returns as repressed content in *The Psychopathology of Everyday Life*, which is full of examples of how the bodies of women make the discourse of man slip. As accurate as the theory of hysteria may be, there is still more to the meaning of the female body. And where the female body signifies beyond the definitions of hysteria is where, in reference to psychoanalytic theory, it is in danger. It is in danger because the female body that exists beyond theory is what returns to disrupt theoretical discourse and makes theoretical discourse slip; because it does this, it risks punishment. *The Psychopathology of Everyday Life* is a text that seeks to develop a theory of the unconscious based on the idea that unconscious ideas can express themselves in conscious discourse. The slips that illustrate this function tend to take a feminized body, text, or foreign language as the space through which they tell themselves; in this they follow the traditional structure of narrative, which tells itself through a feminine space.[13] This feminine space is a theoretical bridge that makes it possible for men to talk to one another about themselves, to the exclusion of real women, but without being exposed to accusations of homosexuality: their exclusive theoretical attachment to other men is triangulated through the idea of a woman. What I have tried to show in my close readings of some of the anecdotes in *The Psychopathology of Everyday Life*, though, is that some meaning that derives from the repression of the interlocutors' experience of the *body* of a real woman, whether mother or lover, inevitably returns to disrupt the masculine hegemony of their dialogues. Psychoanalytic theory has not explained or contained the possibilities of meaning produced not by women but, rather, by the female body. When this body exceeds the limits inscribed for it, it is in danger, because the man will go to great lengths in order to protect the *idea* of woman that is necessary for his own discourse.

An example of what can happen to real women's bodies that do not comply with the theory of femininity may be found by way of three anecdotes that connect "Fragment of an Analysis of a Case of Hysteria" and *The Psychopathology of Everyday Life*. I have made it a practice in this study to analyze only Freud's Freudian slips, especially as they appear in the first edition of *The Psychopathology of Everyday Life*. Since I think, as I have explained, that the added anecdotes and expanded editions function as a kind of camouflage, I wanted to try to get to what Freud had to say about slips, and how he said it, before he had become a canonical figure. In the context of this part of my argument, the first edition is of specific importance because it is the text that Freud wrote around his "Fragment" about Dora. But there is a clue in the 1919 edition of *The Psychopathology of Everyday Life* that pointed me in the direction of what I want to say about the sometimes deadly collision between theory and women's bodies, and so, by way of explanation, I will include it here. It is an anecdote contributed by Freud's favorite student and then colleague, Sandor Ferenczi:

> "I am reminded of the *Anektode*," I once wrote in my notebook. Naturally I meant *"Anekdote* [anecdote]"; actually it was the one about a Gypsy who had been sentenced to death [*Tode*], and who asked as a favour to be allowed himself to choose the tree from which he was to be hanged. (In spite of a keen search he failed to find any suitable tree.) (125)

This anecdote has in common with slips from the first edition the use of a foreign language (despite German's currency as the official language of the Austro-Hungarian Empire, Ferenczi's "native" tongue was Magyar) and a context in which the fate of the body of a feminized and foreign other (the Gypsy) is in question. It is striking because it is about a joke, in which, because of an adept manipulation of language, the Gypsy may have to live under, but will never actually suffer, the death sentence. So this *anekTode* is not about death but, rather, about survival.

Nevertheless, the term *anekTode* pursues the reader and writer. Freud juxtaposed Ferenczi's story with another one that he added in the 1917 edition, in which a doctor three times prescribes deadly overdoses of belladonna to elderly women whom, he unconsciously perceived, had inhibited his erotic relationships with younger women. Derrida alludes to this series of anecdotes in *Writing and Difference*, as a way of raising the question of the slip and responsibility in reference to "the murderous *lapsus calami* [slip of the pen]."[14] But these slips of the pen, like Ferenczi's *anekTode*, do not seek to murder just anybody. Both kinds are specifically directed toward foreign bodies: those of old women and Gypsies. When the theoretical pen slips, it threatens feminized bodies with murder.

In the first edition of *The Psychopathology of Everyday Life* Freud tells us that he too once came close to hurting a patient, though the repercussions of his action would not have been deadly. He visited an old woman every morning and had two bottles of medicine prepared for her: one a blue bottle with eye lotion, the other a white bottle with morphine for her daily injection. On the day in question Freud discovered that he had mixed up the bottles and put drops of morphine, instead of lotion, into the woman's eyes. He "was greatly frightened" (177) until he realized that the morphine would not do any harm. Nevertheless, he analyzed his fright since it was an affect that was out of rational proportion to the situation. He came to the conclusion that, however old she may have been, the woman might still be conceived of as a mother, his mother, and that the fright came from the idea of harming—whether by poisoning or having sex with her— "the old woman," who is always identified with the mother. Freud insists on the fact that "of the two possible errors, using the morphine solution for the eye or the eye lotion for the injection, I had chosen by far the more harmless one" (178). This assertion is made in the main part of the text. But, if we turn again to the footnotes, we may gradually discover an instance in which a Freudian slip killed.

In *The Psychopathology of Everyday Life* Freud refers to a physician's misdiagnosis of an ailment as a form of a slip. An example of this kind of misdiagnosis, in a case in which Freud corrected it, appears in "Fragment of an Analysis of a Case of Hysteria" as well. The context for this footnote is the statement in the main part of the text that it is a characteristic of the discourse of hysterics that they cannot "give an ordered history of their life in so far as it coincides with the history of their illness."[15] One of Freud's colleague's sent his sister to Freud to be treated for hysteria, in which she had pains and difficulty walking. What the colleague told Freud "seemed quite consistent with the diagnosis."[16] But, when the woman came to Freud, he asked her in their first hour together

> to tell [him] her story herself. When the story came out perfectly clearly and connectedly in spite of the remarkable events it dealt with, I told myself that the case could not be one of hysteria.[17]

Freud did a physical examination and discovered that the woman was suffering from tabes, which is a syphilitic infection of the spinal cord. The woman was later healed of the tabes because of Freud's intervention; here he saves her body from a misapplication of the theory of hysteria. He could diagnosis her correctly because he could understand her. Her story made sense to him because it fit in with his theory.

Another of Freud's patients was not so fortunate. In the first edition of chapter 7 of *The Psychopathology of Everyday Life*, "The Forgetting of Impressions and Intentions," Freud discusses how in even nonneurotic people "the recollection of distressing impressions and the occurrence of distressing thoughts are opposed by a resistance" (146). Freud supplies an illustrative footnote about how this occurs. "In the days while [he] was engaged in writing these pages," he forgot entirely who a patient mentioned repeatedly in his engagement book was, despite the fact that he had seen the person in a sanatorium every day over a period of weeks. "Could it have been a man, I asked myself, a case of general paralysis, an uninteresting case?" Finally, after looking at his list of payments, he discovered who the patient was. She was a fourteen-year-old girl, who had come to Freud with "an unmistakable hysteria, which did in fact clear up quickly and radically under [his] care." Her parents took her away after this improvement, but

> she still complained of abdominal pains which had played the chief part in the clinical picture of her hysteria. Two months later she died of sarcoma of the abdominal glands. The hysteria, to which she was at the same time predisposed, used the tumour as a provoking cause, and I with my attention held by the noisy but harmless manifestations of the hysteria, had perhaps overlooked the first signs of the insidious and incurable disease. (146 n. 1)

This is the real *anekTode*, because, out of all of the examples that I have mentioned, it is the one in which somebody dies. Freud is careful to point out, by the use of the word *incurable*, that even had he discovered the cancer, he could not have saved the girl's life. But one wonders how the meaning of the girl's life, for *her*, might have been different if her own body, in addition to the doctor's theory, had been received as more meaningful discourse.

The mistake is not the diagnosis of hysteria, it is that *the diagnosis of hysteria precludes other meanings*. The effect of a diagnosis of hysteria, given in the cultural context of the twentieth century, whether at Freud's end of it or ours, is precisely to undermine the possibility of entering into dialogue with a discourse that proceeds from a female body. I am trying to avoid the obfuscations introduced by suggestions about *écriture féminine*, or notions of reading, writing, or thinking with and through the body. Questions of essentialism or the performance of gender become remarkably irrelevant in moments like those described in *The Psychopathology of Everyday Life:* in a male doctor's consulting room, at the moment of rape, men with power could care less whether femininity and gender are the results of nature or nurture. The female body and what it signifies in the language of male power are what determine how that power acts, or does not act, upon that body. That language of power will always seek to uphold itself. It may confess its mistakes, but only when it is too late for a woman to respond.

In the instance of the girl with cancer Freud says that he asked himself, "Could it have been a man, a case of general paralysis, an uninteresting case?" (146). A male body is here equated with "general paralysis," and both are "uninteresting." A paralyzed body is uninteresting precisely because it will not respond to the physician's proddings. A male body is uninteresting, too, because the doctor has no (conscious) interest in its response, either. The answer to his question is, "No, it could not have been a man." A woman is absolutely necessary to the production of male theory. In this case the idea of her femininity confirms the diagnosis and theory of hysteria. She dies because her body exceeds that theory, and her doctor could not engage with it in its own terms. But some echo of what it was saying comes back, even if in a footnote, to challenge mastery.

There are female bodies that say something that is foreign to hegemonic discourse, and what they say is accorded the same treatment as an inessential foreign language. It is ignored or, at best, becomes a footnote to whatever else is seen as really important. Sometimes what these bodies say is simply that there is more going on with them than what the discourse of power is willing to read or interpret, because that excess is a sign of the fictiveness, or limitations, of dominance. Sometimes they are saying that the discourse of power is killing them by forcing its meanings on them. Freud writes that the case of the hysterical girl with cancer "taught [him] a lesson that [he] is not likely ever to forget" (146 n. 2). The lesson is that a theory that cannot risk learning and using the language of what is foreign to it can kill. It will be murderous when its authority is most threatened by something that exceeds it. The *anekTode* shows the effect of a misogyny trying to eradicate the female body that insists on wreaking havoc with theory, but without which the theory would not exist. It is the story of how theory punishes that which slips past it.

AnekTodes are specifically constructed with the writing of not only

"Fragment of an Analysis of a Case of Hysteria" but also of two other stories about hysteria, because it is in these cases that the female body most obviously exceeds the syntax of the theory that means to explain it; it is where what it signifies is most foreign. The fourteen-year-old girl is cured of her hysteria, but her body goes on to disrupt the writing of *The Psychopathology of Everyday Life*. The footnote about her starts, "In the days while I was writing these pages..."; the outcome of the incident cost the author "moments of the greatest distress" (146). The girl who was not hysterical, but only syphilitic, whom Freud astutely cured of tabes in a footnote to the "Fragment of an Analysis of a Case of Hysteria," is an obvious corrective to the story of the hysterical girl he did *not* cure. The autonomy of the female body, such as it is, redirects the writer's attention and the form of his discourse. This is especially true for Dora, who took her body away. Like the Gypsy who never found a proper tree to be hanged from, Dora did not die under the sentence of theory. She left. Her leaving altered the structure and history of publication of a theoretical text, "Fragment of an Analysis of a Case of Hysteria," and influenced the writing of another book, *The Psychopathology of Everyday Life*. Try as he might to keep it unpublished, the "Fragment of an Analysis of a Case of Hysteria" finds its way into *The Psychopathology of Everyday Life*.

Another way that this happens is in the form of a slip. In a footnote added to the Dora case in 1923 Freud writes that "the treatment described in this paper was broken off on December 31st, 1899. My account of it was written during the two weeks immediately following, but was not published until 1905."[18] Strachey gently brackets the comment "[This should be '1900.' See p. 5]." On that page, in his editor's note, Strachey says:

It is curious that three times in his later writing Freud assigns his treatment of "Dora" to the wrong year—to 1899 instead of 1900. The mistake occurs in the first section of his "History of the Psycho-Analytic Movement" (1914*d*) and is repeated twice in the footnote which he added to the case history in 1923 (p. 13 *n*). There can be no question that the autumn of 1900 was the correct date, since, quite apart from the external evidence quoted above, the date is absolutely fixed by the "1902" given at the end of the paper itself (p. 122).[19]

The connection between the Freudian slip and the Dora case is so durable that it persists for almost twenty-five years after the writing of both texts and is now enshrined in the editorial material of the *Standard Edition*. To misdate something is to err about its most elemental factual content, that is, when it occurred. When Freud gets the date wrong in this parapraxis, he is doing what he claims hysterics do with their narratives of their life histories:

> The sequence of different events is uncertain. Even during the course of their story patients will repeatedly correct a particular or a date, and then perhaps, after wavering for some time, return to their original version.[20]

This statement is the context in which the story about the girl with tabes is told; it is a point of direct connection between the writing of theory, the female body, and the way that its foreignness derails that writing and frequently produces in it the same symptoms that it is trying to describe. Hysteria, like parapraxis, is contagious.

Slipping up with the date of Dora is where a trace of *The Psychopathology of Everyday Life* may be seen in the "Fragment." The most obvious spot where what will be the "Fragment" is visible in the book on slips is in the anecdote about the name Dora that I mentioned at the beginning of this chapter. It appears in the first edition of *The Psychopathology of Everyday Life* and explains how Freud came to choose the name Dora for his (at that time unpublished) case history. As noted, many critics have explicated this anecdote in reference to the "Fragment"; my point here is simply to indicate that Freud could not keep Dora out of print, no matter how much he resisted publishing the case and no matter for what reasons. She had to appear because she is the theoretical incarnation of the slip itself; she is that which is constructed as foreign and feminine and which inevitably will assert itself in discourses that seek to repress it.

Of course, this textual incarnation is only tangentially related to the female body upon which it is distantly founded. Dora is not the female patient's real name. Before she can make even a disruptive appearance, she undergoes a process of rewriting; she "cannot keep her own name" (241). The names that women have for themselves must remain foreign and untranslated in theory, because to say them as they are will alter reality. If Freud had written directly about Ida

Bauer, he would have been attacking the rules of the medical profession and all of the structures of bourgeois society that insist upon privacy and confidentiality. He could have written the same theory, but his authority would be in question because his writing did not participate in polite and official social structures; it would have caused a scandal. These social structures, whether the politesse of middle-class fin de siècle Vienna or the rituals and limits of various professional markets, shiver before difference and do not learn its languages. In particular, the female body, as epitomized by a woman's name before a theoretical rewriting, is a constant reminder of an alternative way of making meaning. It suggests the possibility of a difference that operates according to its own rules and exceeds the mastery of official discourse.

I have said, in answer to Freud's question "Could it have been a man?" that, no, it had to be a woman who functioned as the catalyst for the slip. The slip is written over that which is, in patriarchy, the definition of the foreign: the female body. In this scheme the female body and its significations become, too, the archetype of the foreign language. In other words, the idea of the foreign is built over a perception of sexual difference, in which that which is masculine is self and that which is feminine other, or that which is masculine is home and that which is feminine is foreign. It is this way of thinking that makes the uncanny, for example, possible.[21] These beliefs strongly affect and determine the meaning of the terms *mother tongue* and *foreign tongue*. But before I begin an analysis of those terms I want to situate what I have to say in the context of psychoanalytic theories of subjectivity, language, and sexual difference.

The existing theory is that the small child begins to use language at the same time that it becomes conscious of the absences of the mother. The child uses words to symbolize, and to ask for, that which it does not have. Words stand in for what is missing: a word is not the thing it stands for; it is a substitute. And at the beginning of this symbolic stage the thing that a word stands for is the mother's body, over whose movements the child has discovered it has no control. Words as symbols allay the child's anxiety during the times that the mother is gone.

The awareness of the mother's absence also indicates to the child that it and the mother are not one: the child discovers that it is separate from the mother. But, as soon as it can call itself by its own name, the child is also aware of the fact that it does not coincide exactly with that name; the name is standing in for the lost unity that the child had before it was aware of itself as separate from the mother. Around this same time the child becomes aware of the presence of the father, or of the father function (those social constructs that act as or in the place of the father), and that the father has something that the mother does not have—in various theories, the penis, the phallus, or just plain power. If the child is a boy, he fears being reduced to her castrated state; if a girl, she has to find a way around it and get what she is missing by getting a man.[22] Because of all of these transactions, which are enforced, however automatically, in our still patriarchal society the female body becomes the emblem of loss and failure. The female body, originally the body of the mother, and thus everybody's original home, should, in terms of chronological priority, be the etymology of all future meaning. But at the moment of the acknowledgment of castration, which is the same moment as the acknowledgment of sexual difference and of the accession into language, the mother's female body becomes foreign, uncanny.

For people who are looking for ways that might permit women to determine the meaning of their female bodies, instead of having them predetermined by existing social structures that devalue and seek to control them, this history of the beginning of language and subjectivity has been a difficult problem. It is allied to the questions of how to get past misogyny while living in patriarchy, or how to get past the misogynist potential of psychoanalysis while still working within its theories, which often seem very accurately to describe psychic and social realities.

I would like to suggest a political practice modeled on the analogy of the mother and foreign tongues. First, one must ask if the mother tongue even exists. Can we hear it or write it or speak it? Or is it a romanticized shield that keeps us from confronting the fact that the language and sign systems that we use are really always—because of the castration that helped us learn to use symbols—the father's tongue? Castration, the dictionary that begins with the phallus, is our first language, if not our native, or mother, tongue. It is not possible to obliterate the history of castration from consciousness; all that can be done in that direction is to repress it, which is to continue to fictionalize (and fear) the female body by way of fetishism. But that castration is our first language does not mean that it is the only one. It is possible to listen to what seems foreign—what exceeds the meanings imposed by castration—to learn its languages, and to do so even without a dictionary. Further, it is a well-known fact that the frequent use of foreign languages inevitably inflects or alters the use of the native tongue. The practice of foreign languages eventually changes the very structure of the first language. If we can practice articulating that which makes sense to us beyond the definitions of castration, our multilingual writing and speaking will effect the radical shift of signifier that Lacan refers to and, with it, change the way that meaning is made.

In this regard, in order to learn to speak something other than patriarchy while still in it, it might be useful to remember that the female body has a discernible meaning that precedes castration; this sense is a reminder that, while the separation from the mother's body may be essential to the accession to language, it should be possible, in theory, to symbolize that loss without the second step of devaluing the mother's body specifically as castrated, that is, as deviating from a prior and superior male form. Castration anxiety is an infantile fear. Belief in castration is an infantile fantasy; it may have made us what we are, but it does not have to continue to be our only point of reference. It should be possible to posit an etymology for castration that has the female body, as original body, at its root. If we can do this, we can remind ourselves that the female is more than foreign and more than home.

The writing of a theory of the unconscious in *The Psychopathology of Everyday Life* travels both consciously and unconsciously, to and from the female body, configuring it as foreign but then finding itself coming out of it. By following the book's slips, it is possible to learn that the foreign tongue will always lead back to the native tongue— that that which is foreign is usually about home and that what seems native is really an artificial language. *The Psychopathology of Everyday Life* teaches that all languages, including the native tongue, are foreign; that once you learn a language it can no longer be foreign to you at all; and that the writing of theory is a round trip.

Epilogue

"sangre en las manos"

This book has been mostly a traditional academic effort—I wrote it to help insure that I would not perish in the tenure process—and, despite some radical opinions and interpretations expressed in it, it follows, more or less, the norms of academic critical writing in the United States in 1995. In the middle of its writing, however, just after the first anniversary of my mother's death from lung cancer, which itself interrupted my ability to write, I had a dream that slipped in and wanted to interrupt its canonical progress.

I am writing this part of this book with a fountain pen. Although this is my normal method of composition, I found during the writing of *Freudian Slips* that I was incapable of putting pen to paper. For the first time I composed a book entirely on a computer, a practice I had formerly detested. But, when I decided to make notes toward this conclusion today, I found that it was easy and necessary to do so by hand.

The dream came when I was, in terms of the total length of the project, halfway through the writing of the book. Instead of traveling from New York to New Jersey to see my psychoanalyst, I had arranged for a telephone conference so as not to lose most of a day's writing to the commute. I told her the dream, which I had had the night before, over the phone, and I am indebted to her for insisting, once again, upon the personal and the obvious.

I dreamed that I was in a classroom and that I was standing at the blackboard. I was the professor (I am a professor), but the other people in the room were not subordinate to me. I was espousing one of my favorite theories, that all traditional narrative depends somewhere upon a dead woman. I wanted to write on the blackboard, "All narrative has blood on its hands." I don't know if I wrote those words down in English or not. I do know that, because the class was made up of both English and Spanish speakers, I did what I sometimes do, in real life, when I am putting up a new and difficult concept or word: I wanted to express it in both languages, and so I began writing in Spanish with chalk on the blackboard. I could feel the chalk on my hand.

The first word on the board was *sangre,* the Spanish word for "blood." Next I wrote *en,* "on." I was about to write *sus,* when I remembered that in Spanish "its," "your," or "my" hands are "the" hands, so I began to write *los,* the masculine article. Before I wrote more than *l,* though, I remembered that, although *mano,* hand, ends with an *o,* it is a feminine, not a masculine, noun. I finished writing *las manos,* relieved that I had gotten it right.

I learned Spanish in the classroom; no one in my family used it, but my mother did tell me that she had studied it for a year or two in junior high school. In fourth grade I was moved from my regular elementary school to a program for gifted children called "Opportunity." Our small city in Pennsylvania had decided that this group would start the study of foreign languages in fourth grade, instead of seventh grade, as was then the custom. There was a Spanish teacher available, and so we began to learn Spanish from a patient, smart woman. I continued with Spanish all the way through high school, not consciously out of love but mainly because the wisdom emanating from the guidance counselor's office was that, the more years of language we had, the better were our chances of getting into a prestigious college and of being awarded financial aid.

As it turned out, I was accepted by the only place I applied to, one of the Seven Sisters women's colleges. I wanted to be an archaeologist, so I took no Spanish my freshman year. Nevertheless, the rigorous language requirement (two years of two languages or one language to the most advanced level of literature courses) hung over my head. We had to take Greek if we wanted to major in archaeology. Unfortunately, my dreams of the Aegean faded as I sank into the whirlpool of Greek verbs, and I had to withdraw from the class. The next year, I reasoned, I would start Spanish again and keep going with it until I fulfilled the requirement.

About this time my best friend and I were reaching our maximum moment of symbiosis. She had a strong family and cultural background in Spanish, and her urgings, combined with my affection for and identification with her, led me finally to choose to major in Spanish. I was good at literary analysis and progressed in my knowledge of Spanish renaissance prose. I went to Spain for the first time in the summer of my junior year. While I was there, my paternal grandmother (the one who quoted Goethe), who had been in many ways the most stabilizing and reliable fixture of my youth, died. I could not get a ticket home for the funeral, so I burned candles in a parish church in the Madrid neighborhood of Chamberí instead.

My senior year passed in a haze of overwrought emotion and academic overwork. Shortly before graduation I ran into my old Greek teacher, who asked what I had majored in. When I told her Spanish, she said, "I wouldn't have thought that languages were your forte." I won a prize in literature and planned to go to graduate school in medieval studies (I had since learned Latin and French) after a year off. When that time came the Ivy League medieval studies department I had applied to could not match the huge (it was the beginning of the 1980s) grants that two other Spanish departments offered, so I went off to Harvard to study the literature of medieval and renaissance Spain.

Many of my friends there were feminists from the French section—it was a Romance languages, not a Spanish, department. After working as a research assistant for a professor who was finishing a book on French feminist theory, the idea occurred to me to do a study of some important works of the Spanish renaissance from the perspective of mostly French feminist theory. No one had ever done this, so it struck me that it might be "the original contribution to knowledge" that a dissertation was supposed to be. Unfortunately, the brilliant and kind male luminary I had gone there to study with died suddenly of a heart attack. Another Olympian, who left the university to retire soon after, called the work "derivative." The only other person in the program told me that it was impossible to write such a thesis in that department at that time and that maybe I should consider doing a dissertation on the love letters of Lope de Vega, which was, according to him, a better topic for a woman.

I fled to the best reader of texts I knew, with whom I had a connection by way of the comparative literature program. She said that she would direct the thesis, and she did. Having worked with her helped me get a job at an East Coast research university. I published the thesis as a book, and now I teach graduate and undergraduate courses in Spanish literature, comparative literature, and women's studies. So, like many of the characters in the anecdotes in *The Psycho-pathology of Everyday Life*, I am a person of academic background, and my discourse participates in some structures of authority.

Also like those other persons of academic background, my profession offers me endless opportunities to commit slips—most of my courses are taught entirely in Spanish, and I sometimes find myself committing slips on easy constructions—or correcting myself just in time. Of course, like every other nonnative and native speaker, I also commit errors of ignorance. But here I'm writing about slips, that is, mistakes you make when you know better. Nancy K. Miller writes about a somewhat similar set of circumstances in her essay "The French Mistake."[1] Miller mentions the specific anxiety produced in the non–native French speaker around the issue of making gender mistakes. She tells the story of a lecturer who says "*le forêt*" (instead of *la*) in his talk. The audience is mortified. Years later Miller decides to tell the anecdote to another group of people. But when she gets to the punch line she herself can no longer remember whether it is *le* or *la forêt*. She confesses her problem to the group after "having made—while *speaking English*—a gender mistake" (51). Why was Miller telling the anecdote in the first place? She says that she does not know. But from experience I can say that one does derive a secret, aggressive pleasure from other peoples' mistakes; it grants a paradoxical kind of authority to one's own: this is why I am telling Miller's story of her own mistake made while telling the story of someone else's. Also, terror consoles itself with (it doesn't love) company.

> *Le* or *la*? It is as though much of the category of gender brings back its total arbitrariness: is the forest masculine or feminine? . . . I am having a full-fledged gender panic attack. (51)

Anxiety fills the article(s), and at one point Miller says that, when she was teaching French in high school, she got "through the day alternating between Valium and Ritalin" (54). The themes of error, gender, and anxiety permeate the essay, and they are present in my dream as well, along with more ominous currents. If it was masochistic for Miller to put herself through what was for her the misery of speaking French, then it is also sadistic to recount the errors of others; even without naming them, there is pleasure in turning them on the spit of correction.

It is possible to make gender mistakes in Spanish, but generally it is harder to do than in French, for example, because gender is more clearly marked in more Spanish nouns than in French ones. Almost every Spanish noun that ends in *o* is masculine; almost every one that ends in *a* is feminine. Words that end in *a* and are masculine are more frequent than those that end in *o* and are feminine. So, my dream had to work hard to produce its dilemma.

Another point of difference between Spanish and French is one allied to gender; Spanish and French have different political valences in the academic culture of the United States. Even at the most elementary level of literature classes in Spanish, it is almost certain that there will be many students who are native speakers of Spanish. This semester, for instance, at Rutgers, I have thirty-one students in my section of the introductory course "Main Currents in Spanish Literature," and about a third of them are native speakers with varying degrees of competence in writing and reading Spanish; in other words, I have freshmen who are "better" (because of their definition as "native," as opposed to "nonnative," or even the strange term "near-native," speakers) at some aspect of my subject that I am. Having students who are better than we are is sometimes a dream of professors, who envision a brilliant graduate student, perhaps, in this role, a freshly minted peer who can teach us as much as we could teach her or him. But the quotidian reality of a student who is technically better (in terms of accent, perhaps) is probably only the fate of teachers of and in foreign languages. The political difference between French and Spanish in most areas of the United States (leaving aside parts of Maine or Louisiana, where, e.g., there are many native French speakers) is based on this difference—that a nonnative professor of Spanish is much more likely to find herself in an economy in which the claim to authority is more problematic than in other classroom situations. The benefit of this is that, if it can be accepted as a reality and not avoided or repressed, it can make for a more dialogic classroom environment, one in which learning, rather than authority, is the paramount concern.

Another difference that distinguishes Spanish from French is historical. English-speaking North Americans have a long history of colonizing Spanish-speaking Americans. English is the language of power in the United States. This historical reality metamorphoses in a classroom such as the one that I have described. Native speakers of Spanish, even if they are not the majority of the students, occupy a position of authority because it is easier for them to speak up, because they know the language of authority. Paradoxically, it is the language that the non–native Spanish-speaking professor is using and upon which basis they will be graded; it is the language of their value in a particular academic market called the Spanish class. The non–native Spanish-speaking students find the balance of power in the classroom, then, not against them—but, probably for the first time, not in their favor. They look at me and see an Anglo professor, but the professor is speaking the language of a group that they see as *other* in a way that a white Anglo college student does not see a French person, or the French language, as other. The native Spanish speakers find themselves in a position in which their discourse is valued as authoritative within a system that elsewhere perpetuates its disenfranchisement. The Anglo students learn that they must use the language of an other in order to claim a new kind of agency. So, the particular political value I have noticed in my classroom at Rutgers is that all the students can learn that discourses of authority, like gender, are not natural but, rather, arbitrary, that everyone is entitled to work their way through their errors and to make meaning.

This is why, when I am teaching and find I have to introduce a new term, like *genre,* for example, I sometimes write the word in both English and Spanish on the blackboard. *Genre* is an interesting example, because it is a French word that has passed into English with only a specific literary meaning; in Spanish, *género* keeps the double meaning of "genre" and (grammatical) "gender" that the French word has. In my dream I don't know if I was teaching a Spanish class, but I do know that, for me, *all* teaching has become a bilingual, and often a multilingual, experience. One language is not enough to respond to the realities and demands of any pedagogy, precisely because of the way that using more than one language, from more than one position in political hierarchies, rebuilds structures of power.

I am a white person from a middle-class family who has benefited from the financial support of wealthy private institutions and I have a strong investment in the reconfiguration of power. I know what it is to be oppressed and limited because of the ways that I do not fit in with or cannot accept established definitions of femininity, for example. To put my authority, such as it is, into discourse in more than one language effects the kind of remaking of relationships that I have been describing. So, in the dream, to write in Spanish is a way of inscribing that new relationship.

Needless to say, all of this talk of the political leads to the personal, and *sangre* (blood) is the most personal thing of all, especially for a woman. This blood also marks a connection with the theoretical argument of this book, which is that Freud writes his theory of parapraxis over the bodies of women. In the *aliquis* chapter, the first one that treats the misquotation of a literary text in a foreign language, the slip is traced back precisely to a woman's blood, to her menstrual period. Most of my book is about how Freud writes around and about women, but I think that my dream might be a useful way of seeing how a woman writes about herself. I wanted to write that "all narrative has blood on its hands," because it is written over women's bodies, but all that came out in Spanish was *"sangre en las manos."* While I was writing the main part of this book, it must have occurred to me that not only does narrative have blood on its hands but so does theory. And I was writing theory about women's bodies.

The interesting thing about the construction *"sangre en las manos"* is that it does not specify whose hands the blood is on. True, I had thought it was on narrative's hands, but what I wrote meant more than that: it could mean, blood on narrative's hands, blood on someone or something else's hands, or blood on *my own* hands. I mentioned earlier that, while I was dreaming that I was writing, I could feel the chalk on my hands. Chalk dust is as dry as—a bone. It is so much the opposite of the feeling of blood that it begins to coincide with it.

It—bone and blood on my hands—seems that there is a deadly feeling about writing. In *The Psychopathology of Everyday Life* this feeling surfaces in reference to the *anekTode*—the story of analytical mastery that is underlain by death. The use of Spanish in the dream helped me to inscribe the association of death and writing without necessarily including myself in it. But the ambiguity of the construction did not absolve me, either. (I should note that I am on the thirteenth page of my handwritten text.) The Spanish made it easier to think that my own hands were not bloody, but the trace of responsibility remained.

To have made an elementary mistake like the ones I thought of but did not write—mistakes of pronoun, gender, or idiomatic expression—is part of the activity that is called, in English, "murdering," or "butchering," a language. I wish I could say here that what I almost butchered was a foreign language, but the rest of this book would put the lie to such an assertion: any language that is called foreign leads back immediately to the body of the mother. And, as I mentioned earlier, my mother had learned a little Spanish in high school, so my mistakes would have butchered a mother tongue. Writing *sangre en las manos* in Spanish may have been an attempt at distancing myself from this murderous atmosphere, but it leads right back to that original female body.

Writing in any language may feel murderous. Writing for publication, in particular, may carry this affect, because it is a way of putting one's discourse out in public, away from the safety of home. And the writer may feel that she goes traveling faraway, wherever her writing goes—maybe even too far, or so far that she will not be able to get back. Freud discusses a similar sensation in his late essay "A Disturbance of Memory on the Acropolis."[2] Freud had longed all his life to see the Acropolis, but when he finally arrived there he could not believe it; it was "too good to be true" (242).[3] He had traveled such a long way, or come so far in life, that he felt the need to deny his own progress: "It seems as though the essence of success was to have got further than one's father, and as though to excel one's father was still something forbidden" (22:247). His travels gave him the sensation of having gone too far from whatever part of his identity was bound up with his father. This sensation is close to a fear of having lost the father forever because of something that one has done; that is, it is akin to childhood feelings of omnipotence, in which the child believes that his or her thoughts and wishes can kill. The childish feeling says, "My father is gone because I have left; by leaving I have eradicated him, and now I can't get him back." There is a fear that going away will destroy the father. But a paradoxical remnant of the effect of his experience, one not discussed by Freud, is that it insists on calling the father to mind, of *reminding* Freud of him just at the moment when he fears he has lost him. In terms of learning foreign languages, which is a way of leaving behind the *father* tongue, a similar situation might apply.

I wonder where Freud's mother is in this essay; he does not mention her, perhaps because she was not a part of the associations that surfaced in his self-analysis. But a woman's body is emphatically present in my dream. Writing in any language can seem like going too far; sometimes using a foreign language can be a way to try to get away, to go further, but other times it is a way to stay at home or to deny having made the trip. The phrase *"sangre en las manos"* makes both a departure from and an encounter with that female body possible. There is a fear that the process of writing has murdered it, but no murder has occurred: at least in the dream the phrase is correct. There was a fear that error would murder the language, but that did not happen. And it is important to remember that, despite the feeling of guilt, in terms of a woman touching a woman's body, having blood on your hands does not have to mean that you have killed anybody. In fact, it is very difficult to inhabit a female body and *not* have bloody hands. Women's hands are bloody on a more or less regular basis, for a big part of their lives, as we attend to the flow of blood of our menstrual periods. A woman who touches her own vulva, or those of other women, is going to have bloody hands.

The fear of writing is like the fear of murdering what you touch. English idiom tells us that, if we have blood on our hands, then we are guilty of murder. What we have to remember is that our hands were bloody before the idiom was invented, but not because of murder or castration. The menstrual blood that appears in the *aliquis* chapter, like the blood on the hands in this dream, leads back to an original female body that makes sense before *and* after castration, or before and beyond a patriarchy that seeks to confine it in its own definitions. It is a mother's body, but it is also our own. We will not kill ourselves or our mothers if our writing stays connected to the everyday experience of living in a female body. If Freud was right that women invented the art of weaving on the analogy of their pubic hair,[4] then it is possible, too, that women were the first writers, because of their unavoidable proximity to that indelible marking substance, blood.

Hélène Cixous and others have proposed an *écriture féminine,* a writing with and of the female body, as a way around discourses that control and oppress it, but that project has fallen victim to a kind of mysticism and obfuscation. I am not suggesting writing with bodily fluids. I am suggesting that women may write in ways that do not repeat the murderous stylistics of patriarchy, and that a way to do this is to *describe* and insist upon the everyday experiences of being in a female body, as both subject and object, in writing, in as many languages as we are able.

Mano may look like a masculine noun, but it is not. To write may seem like an activity that belongs to someone else (*sus*) or that pertains and can only pertain to the masculine (*los*) and irrevocably leads to the murder of a female body that exceeds the grammar of femininity. But the idea that my reading and writing will somehow be deadly to me or other women or that the hand that writes cannot be mine—*mano* ends in *o*, so it must be masculine—is contradicted by the action in the dream. Theorizing, like dreaming, is a kind of wish fulfillment that can affect daily reality. In the dream I write, and no one dies; I fear error, but I make more sense than I ever expected to because of it. *"Sangre en las manos"* can be read as the practical epigraph to a theory of feminist meaning.

Notes

Introduction

1. See "The Pretended Aunt" in *Exemplary Novels of Miguel de Cervantes*, trans. Walter K. Kelly (London: H. G. Bohn, 1855). The essay to which I refer is "'The Pretended Aunt': Misreadings and The Scandal of the Missing Mothers," in *Quixotic Desire: Cervantes and Psychoanalysis*, ed. Ruth El Saffar and Diana Wilson (Ithaca: Cornell UP, 1994) 255–63.

Chapter 1

1. *The Complete Letters of Sigmund Freud to Wilhelm Fliess, 1887–1904*, ed. and trans. Jeffrey Moussaieff Masson (Cambridge: Harvard UP, 1985) 427. In further citations this title appears abbreviated as *Letters*.
2. *Letters* 430.
3. Sigmund Freud, *The Psychopathology of Everyday Life*, vol. 6, *The Standard Edition of the Complete Psychological Works of Sigmund Freud*, trans. James Strachey (London: Hogarth Press, 1960) 278. Further page references to Freud's works in the *Standard Edition* are parenthesized in the text as *SE* followed by volume and page numbers. In some close readings, I supply the original German from Sigmund Freud, *Zur Psychopathologie des Alltagslebens* (Frankfurt am Main: Fischer Taschenbuch Verlag, 1954).
4. *Letters* 442.
5. *Letters* 447.
6. Masson, in *Letters* 2–4; 459–60.
7. Sigmund Freud, *The Origins of Psycho-Analysis: Letters to Wilhelm Fliess, Drafts and Notes: 1887–1902*, ed. Marie Bonaparte, Anna Freud, and Ernst Kris; intro. by Ernst Kris (New York: Basic Books, 1954).
8. Avital Ronell cites this quotation from the title page of *The Psychopathology of Everyday Life* at the beginning of part 1 of her book *Dictations: On Haunted Writing* (Bloomington: Indiana UP, 1986), to give an indication of how "the *Psychopathology* is spooked" by Goethe and how Goethe is a kind of ghostwriter in Freud. The book does not mention Freud's slip and discusses issues other than parapraxis.

9. For complete explanations of male homosocial desire and *hom(m)osexualité*, see Eve K. Sedgwick, *Between Men: English Literature and Homosocial Desire* (New York: Columbia UP, 1985); and Luce Irigaray, *Speculum of the Other Woman*, trans. Gillian C. Gill (Ithaca: Cornell UP, 1985), first published in French by Editions de Minuit, 1974.

10. *Letters* 447.

11. Ernest Jones, *The Life and Work of Sigmund Freud*, 3 vols. (New York: Basic Books, 1953) 1:317. Further references will be to Jones, *Life*, followed by volume and page number.

12. *The Psychopathology of Everyday Life* 144 n. 1; Jones, *Life*, 1:314.

13. German quotations from *Faust* are from Walter Kaufmann's facing translation: Johann Wolfgang von Goethe, *Goethe's Faust* (New York: Doubleday/Anchor, 1961–1963) 457. English translations are as literal as I could make them.

14. Jacques Derrida, "Freud and the Scene of Writing," *Writing and Difference*, trans. Alan Bass (Chicago: University of Chicago Press, 1978) 230. The roman and arabic numerals in the quotation refer to the *Standard Edition*.

15. See pages 85–86 of the present study.

16. Sebastiano Timpanaro, *The Freudian Slip: Psychoanalysis and Textual Criticism*, trans. Kate Soper (London: NLB, 1976); and James Guetti, "Freudian Slippage" *Raritan* 8 (Summer 1988): 36–58.

17. The quotation from *The Merchant of Venice* (*Psychopathology of Everyday Life*, 97–98) is an example.

18. NBC Channel 4 news broadcast, 5 P.M., Friday, 23 October 1992, New York; and NBC's "Saturday Night Live," "Weekend Update" with Kevin Nealon, 24 October 1992.

19. "Constructions in Analysis," *SE* 23:255–70. Neither Timpanaro nor Guetti mention this essay.

20. Anthony Wilden, "Lacan and the Discourse of the Other," in Jacques Lacan, *Speech and Language in Psychoanalysis*, trans. Anthony Wilden (Baltimore: Johns Hopkins UP, 1968) 247–49, 265–66. Jane Gallop, *Reading Lacan* (Ithaca: Cornell UP, 1985) 39–44.

21. Shoshona Felman, *The Literary Speech Act: Don Juan with J. L. Austin, or Seduction in Two Languages*, trans. Catharine Porter (Ithaca: Cornell UP, 1983) 117–22, 138.

22. Barbara Johnson, "Teaching Ignorance: L'Ecole des Femmes," *A World of Difference* (Baltimore: Johns Hopkins UP, 1987) 68–85.

23. Teresa de Lauretis, "Desire in Narrative," *Alice Doesn't: Feminism, Semiotics, Cinema* (Bloomington: Indiana UP, 1984) 103–57.

Chapter 2

1. For a complete list of the editions and dates of *The Psychopathology of Everyday Life*, see the editor's introduction, *SE* 6:ix. I discuss the multiplicity of editions and additions to the work on pages 75–79 of the present study.

2. Examples of other slips that Freud did not intend for publication appear in his letters to Fliess; see Ernst Kris, introduction to Sigmund Freud, *The Origins of Psycho-Analysis: Letters to Wilhelm Fliess, Drafts and Notes: 1887–1902*, ed. Marie Bonaparte, Anna Freud, and Ernst Kris (New York: Basic Books, 1954); and *The Complete Letters*

of Sigmund Freud to Wilhelm Fliess, 1887–1904, ed. and trans. Jeffrey Moussaieff (Cambridge: Harvard UP, 1985).

3. Peter Gay, *Freud: A Life for Our Time* (New York: Norton, 1988) 138–39.

4. *Erfahren, Zur Psychopathologie des Alltagslebens,* 19.

5. Although he does not emphasize the aspect of the feminization of the foreign, in *Orientalism* (New York: Random House, 1978), Edward Said explains how academic discourses can be used to maintain power over "foreign" others.

6. Audre Lorde, "The Master's Tools Will Never Dismantle the Master's House," *Sister Outsider* (Trumansburg, N.Y.: Crossing Press, 1984) 110–13.

7. One of the friend's associations is to Simon of Trent. He says that he is "thinking of the accusation of ritual blood-sacrifice which is being brought against the Jews again just now, and of *Kleinpaul's* book [1892] in which he regards all these supposed victims as incarnations, one might say new editions, of the Saviour" (*SE* 6:10).

8. In "The Politics of Interpretations" (in *In Other Worlds: Essays in Cultural Politics* [New York: Routledge, 1988]) Gayatri Spivak notes that it is "at those borders of discourse where metaphor and example seem arbitrarily *chosen* that ideology breaks through" (125). The examples that I list here all pertain explicitly and specifically to current (Spring 1995) political problems and identifications of groups whose fate I feel my own is intimately bound up with.

9. Monique Wittig, "On the Social Contract," in *The Straight Mind and Other Essays* (Boston: Beacon Press, 1992) 42.

Chapter 3

1. Susie Bright, "Undressing Camille," in *Susie Bright's Sexual Reality: A Virtual Sex World Reader* (Pittsburgh: Cleis Press, 1992) 74.

2. See the "Index of Parapraxes," *SE* 6:291–96, for a list of the slips that indicate how many involve female or feminized bodies that exceed male control.

3. The word play originates in the German original: "Gut, da komme ich also auf den lächerlichen Einfall, mir das Wort in folgender Art zu zerteilen: *a* und *liquis.*" Was soll das?—"Weiss ich nicht."—Was fällt Ihnen weiter dazu ein?—"Das setzt sich so fort: Reliquien-Liquidation-Flüssigkeit-Fluid." Wissen Sie jetzt schon etwas? "Nein, noch lange nicht. Aber fahren Sie forte," *Zur Psychopathologie des Alltagslebens* 19.

4. This is the situation of President Schreber, whose repressed homosexuality expressed itself in paranoid fantasies of having a woman's body and giving birth by means of it. See "Psychoanalytic Notes on an Autobiographical Account of a Case of Paranoia (Dementia Paranoides)," *SE* 12:2–82.

5. *Screen Memories* (1899), *SE* 3:301–22.

6. Jones, *Life* 1:13. See also Freud's letters to Fliess.

7. "The Uncanny," *SE* 17:245.

Chapter 4

1. *Zur Psychopathologie des Alltagslebens* 24.

2. Peter Gay, *Freud: A Life for Our Time* (New York: Norton, 1988) 138.

3. Gay, *Freud* 16.

4. "Fetishism," *SE* 21:152.

5. Roland Barthes, *S/Z: An Essay*, trans. Richard Miller (New York: Hill and Wang, 1974) 106–7.

6. See "Fetishism," esp. 153–54.

7. Jacques Lacan, "The Agency of the Letter in the Unconscious or Reason since Freud," *Ecrits*, trans. Alan Sheridan (New York: Norton, 1977) 175.

8. Lacan, "Agency" 157.

9. Barbara Johnson, "Taking Fidelity Philosophically," in *Difference in Translation*, ed. Joseph F. Graham (Ithaca: Cornell UP, 1985) 143–44.

10. Lacan, "Agency" 170.

11. Lacan, "Agency" 170, 174

12. "Kein anderer," *Zur Psychopathologie des Alltagslebens* 145 n. 56.

13. "Lecture Three, Parapraxes, part 2," in *Introductory Lectures on Psycho-Analysis*, *SE* 15:50–51.

14. Jones, *Life*, 1:174–75.

15. Miguel de Cervantes, *Don Quijote de la Mancha* (Barcelona: Editorial Juventud, 1985) 2:863; English translation by J. M. Cohen (New York: Penguin, 1965) 759.

16. Jones, *Life* 1:164.

17. S. B. Vranich, "Sigmund Freud and 'The Case History of Berganza': Freud's Psychoanalytic Beginnings," *Psychoanalytic Review* 63 (1976): 73–82, draws biographical conclusions relevant to Cervantes's text.

18. De Lauretis discusses this in the context of Shoshona Felman's "Rereading Femininity," *Yale French Studies* 62 (1981): 19–21, in "Desire in Narrative," *Alice Doesn't: Feminism, Semiotics, Cinema* (Bloomington: Indiana UP, 1984) 111–12.

Chapter 5

1. "Ich werde mich hier darauf beschränken, einege sorgfältig analysierte Beispiele mitzuteilen, und keinen Versuch unternehmen, das Ganze der Erscheinungen zu umfassen" (*Zur Psychopathologie des Alltagslebens* 88).

2. *Bruchflächen*, *Zur Psychopathologie des Alltagslebens* 217.

3. *The Complete Letters of Sigmund Freud to Wilhelm Fliess, 1887–1904*, ed. and trans. Jeffrey Moussaieff Masson (Cambridge: Harvard UP, 1985) 441. According to Masson's note to this letter, "Freud mocks making the sign of the cross three times to protect oneself from evil" (441 n. 2).

4. I am grateful to Professor Harry Berger of the University of California at Santa Cruz, who was the first person who pointed this etymology out to me.

5. Probably the best place to start exploring the extensive bibliography on "Fragment of an Analysis of a Case of Hysteria" is the critical anthology *In Dora's Case: Freud, Hysteria, Feminism*, ed. Charles Bernheimer and Claire Kahane, 2d ed. (New York: Columbia UP, 1990).

6. For a brief and lucid chronology of the writing of the two works, see the editor's note to "Fragment of an Analysis of a Case of Hysteria" (*SE* 3:3–6). Further detail may be garnered from the Freud-Fliess correspondence (esp. 426–48).

7. *Letters* 433.

8. *Letters* 432.

9. *Letters* 324.

10. *Anecdote, American Heritage Dictionary of the English Language* (New York: Houghton Mifflin, 1973) 49–50.

11. "Fragment of an Analysis of a Case of Hysteria," *SE* 7:39.

12. *American Heritage Dictionary* 521.

13. Teresa de Lauretis, "Desire in Narrative," *Alice Doesn't: Feminism, Semiotics, Cinema* (Bloomington: Indiana UP, 1984) 118–19.

14. Jacques Derrida, "Freud and the Scene of Writing," *Writing and Difference*, trans. Alan Bass (Chicago: University of Chicago Press, 1978) 230.

15. "Fragment" 16.

16. "Fragment" 16 n. 2.

17. "Fragment" 17.

18. "Fragment" 13 n. 1.

19. "Fragment" 5.

20. "Fragment" 16.

21. For a related discussion, please see chapter 3, pp. 55–56, of the present study.

22. This summary is based on ideas in Freud's *Beyond the Pleasure Principle* (*SE* 18) and Jacques Lacan's theories about castration, the relationship to the mother, and the accession to language; for an overview of Lacan's work in this field, see Jacques Lacan, *Feminine Sexuality*, ed. Juliet Mitchell and Jacqueline Rose (New York: Norton, 1982).

Epilogue

1. Nancy K. Miller, "The French Mistake," *Getting Personal: Feminist Occasions and Other Autobiographical Acts* (New York: Routledge, 1991) 48–55.

2. "A Disturbance of Memory on the Acropolis," *SE* 22:239–48.

3. *SE* 22:242

4. "Femininity," *New Introductory Lectures on Psychoanalysis, SE* 22:112–35.

Bibliography

American Heritage Dictionary of the English Language. New York: Houghton Mifflin, 1973.

Barthes, Roland. *S/Z: An Essay*. Trans. Richard Miller. New York: Hill and Wang, 1974.

Bernheimer, Charles and Kahane, Claire. *In Dora's Case: Freud, Hysteria, Feminism*. Second edition. New York: Columbia University Press, 1990.

Bright, Susie. *Susie Bright's Sexual Reality: A Virtual Sex World Reader*. Pittsburgh: Cleis Press, 1992.

Cervantes Saavedra, Miguel de. *Don Quijote de la Mancha*. 2 vols. Ed. Martin de Riquer. Barcelona: Editorial Juventud, 1985.

———. *Don Quixote*. Trans. J. M. Cohen. New York: Penguin, 1965.

———. "The Pretended Aunt." In *Exemplary Novels of Miguel de Cervantes*. Trans., Walter K. Kelly. London: H. G. Bohn, 1855.

de Lauretis, Teresa. *Alice Doesn't: Feminism, Semiotics, Cinema*. Bloomington: Indiana University Press, 1984.

Derrida, Jacques. *Writing and Difference*. Trans. Alan Bass. Chicago: University of Chicago Press, 1978.

Felman, Shoshona. "Rereading Femininity." *Yale French Studies* 62 (1981), 19–44.

———. *The Literary Speech Act: Don Juan with J. L. Austin, or Seduction in Two Languages*. Trans. Catharine Porter. Ithaca: Cornell University Press, 1983.

Freud, Sigmund. *The Standard Edition of the Complete Psychological Works of Sigmund Freud*. 23 vols. Ed. and Trans. James Strachey. London: The Hogarth Press, 1960.

———. *Zur Psychopathologie des Alltagslebens*. Frankfurt: Fischer Taschenbuch, 1990 (1954).

———. *The Origins of Psycho-Analysis: Letters to Wilhelm Fliess, Drafts and Notes: 1887–1902*. Ed. Marie Bonaparte, Anna Freud, and Ernst Kris. Introduction by Ernst Kris. New York: Basic Books, 1954.

Freud, Sigmund and Fliess, Wilhelm. *The Complete Letters of Sigmund Freud to Wilhelm Fliess 1887–1904*. Ed. and Trans. Jeffrey Moussaieff Masson. Cambridge: Harvard University Press, 1985.

Gallop, Jane. *Reading Lacan*. Ithaca: Cornell University Press, 1985.

Gay, Peter. *Freud: A Life for Our Time*. New York: Norton, 1988.

Goethe, Johann Wolfgang von. *Goethe's Faust*. Bilingual edition. Trans. Walter Kaufman. New York: Doubleday/Anchor, 1961/1963.

Gossy, Mary S. "'The Pretended Aunt': Misreadings and the Scandal of the Missing

Mothers." In *Quixotic Desire: Psychoanalytic Perspectives on Cervantes*. Ed. Ruth A. El Saffar and Diana D. Wilson. Ithaca: Cornell University Press, 1993, 255–63.

Guetti, James. "Freudian Slippage." *Raritan* 8 (1988), 36–58.

Irigaray, Luce. *Speculum of the Other Woman*. Trans. Gillian C. Gill. Ithaca: Cornell University Press, 1985. (First French edition, Paris: Editions de Minuit, 1974.)

Johnson, Barbara. "Taking Fidelity Philosophically." In *Difference in Translation*. Ed. Joseph F. Graham. Ithaca: Cornell University Press, 1985, 142–48.

———. "Teaching Ignorance: *L'Ecole des Femmes*." In *A World of Difference*. Ed. Barbara Johnson. Baltimore: Johns Hopkins University Press, 1987, 68–85.

Jones, Ernest. *The Life and Work of Sigmund Freud*. 3 vols. New York: Basic Books, 1953.

Lacan, Jacques. *Speech and Language in Psychoanalysis*. Trans. Anthony Wilden. Baltimore: Johns Hopkins University Press, 1968.

———. *Ecrits*. Trans. Alan Sheridan. New York: Norton, 1977.

———. *Feminine Sexuality*. Eds. Juliet Mitchell and Jacqueline Rose. New York: Norton, 1982.

Lorde, Audre. *Sister Outsider*. Trumansburg, N.Y.: The Crossing Press, 1984.

Miller, Nancy K. *Getting Personal: Feminist Occasions and Other Autobiographical Acts*. New York: Routledge, 1991.

Ronell, Avital. *Dictations: On Haunted Writing*. Bloomington: Indiana University Press, 1986.

Said, Edward. *Orientalism*. New York: Random House, 1978.

Sedgwick, Eve K. *Between Men: English Literature and Homosocial Desire*. New York: Columbia University Press, 1985.

Spivak, Gayatri Chakravorty. *In Other Worlds: Essays in Cultural Politics*. New York: Routledge, 1988.

Timpanaro, Sebastiano. *The Freudian Slip: Psychoanalysis and Textual Criticism*. Trans. Kate Soper. London: NLB, 1976.

Vranich, S. B. "Sigmund Freud and 'The Case History of Berganza': Freud's Psychoanalytic Beginnings." *Psychoanalytic Review* 63 (1976), 73–82.

Wilden, Anthony. "Lacan and the Discourse of the Other." In Lacan, *Speech and Language*, 159–311.

Wittig, Monique. *The Straight Mind and Other Essays*. Boston: Beacon Press, 1992.